IMPROVE YOUR MEMORY

SIXTH EDITION

Ron Fry

Course Technology PTR

A part of Cengage Learning

COURSE TECHNOLOGY
CENGAGE Learning™

Australia, Brazil, Japan, Korea, Mexico, Singapore, Spain, United Kingdom, United States

COURSE TECHNOLOGY
CENGAGE Learning™

Improve Your Memory,
Sixth Edition
Ron Fry

Publisher and General Manager,
Course Technology PTR:
Stacy L. Hiquet

Associate Director of
Marketing:
Sarah Panella

Manager of Editorial Services:
Heather Talbot

Marketing Manager:
Mark Hughes

Senior Acquisitions Editor:
Mitzi Koontz

Interior Layout Tech:
Judy Littlefield

Cover Designer:
Luke Fletcher

Indexer:
Larry D. Sweazy

Proofreader:
Sandi Wilson

For product information and technology assistance, contact us at **Cengage Learning Customer &**
Sales Support, 1-800-354-9706

For permission to use material from this text or product, submit all requests online at **cengage.com/permissions**
Further permissions questions can be e-mailed to
permissionrequest@cengage.com.

All trademarks are the property of their respective owners.

All images © Cengage Learning unless otherwise noted.

Library of Congress Control Number: 2011930895

ISBN-13: 978-1-4354-6110-9

ISBN-10: 1-4354-6110-X

Course Technology, a part of Cengage Learning
20 Channel Center Street
Boston, MA 02210
USA

Cengage Learning is a leading provider of customized learning solutions with office locations around the globe, including Singapore, the United Kingdom, Australia, Mexico, Brazil, and Japan. Locate your local office at:
international.cengage.com/region.

Cengage Learning products are represented in Canada by Nelson Education, Ltd.

For your lifelong learning solutions, visit **courseptr.com.**

Visit our corporate Web site at **cengage.com.**

Printed by RR Donnelley.
Crawfordsville, IN. 1st Ptg. 06/2011

Printed in the United States of America
1 2 3 4 5 6 7 13 12 11

CONTENTS

FOREWORD

SOMETHING TO REMEMBER

If it weren't for the fact that reading is the absolute underpinning of every other study skill, I could make a pretty strong case that spending time improving your memory would deliver the most "study bang" for the buck. It doesn't matter how rapidly you whiz through your textbooks if you can't even remember the subject you just studied five minutes later. Getting organized is essential, but not too effective if you always forget to carry your calendar and regularly turn in homework assignments late. And, of course, spending hours searching high and low for keys, glasses, and other essentials isn't exactly the most efficient way to start your study day.

As important as they are, basic memory techniques are the study ingredients least likely to be taught in schools, even in a study skills course. So while the better schools and teachers might help you with reading, writing, organizing, and test strategies, far too many of them will "forget" to help you with your memory...or to find your glasses, keys, etc.

This small book will give you so many easy ways to remember more, you'll wonder why you didn't become a "memorist" years ago.

I am proud that I have been helping students of all ages improve their study skills ever since the day I walked into a bookstore and realized there was no single book then available that simply taught someone how to study! This year marks another major milestone in the more than 20-year-long evolution of my *How to Study Program*—the reissuance of new editions of all the volumes in the series: *How to Study, Improve Your Memory, Improve Your Reading, Improve Your Writing, Ace Any Test,* and *Get Organized.*

My readers are far more varied than I ever expected. A number of you are students, not just the high school students I always thought were my readers, but also college students, who are making up for study skills you missed in high school, and junior high school students, who are trying to master these study skills early in your school career to maximize your opportunities for success.

Some readers are adults returning to school who have figured out that if you can learn now what your teachers never taught you the first time around, you will do better in your careers. Wouldn't it be great to recall without notes the key points you want to make in your presentation, or remember the names of all the potential new clients you just met at a cocktail party?

All too many of you are parents with the same lament: "How do I get Jill to do better in school? She can't remember my birthday, let alone when her next trigonometry test is."

If you are still in high school, you will have no problem with the language and format of this book—its relatively short sentences and paragraphs, humorous (hopefully) headings and subheadings, and reasonable but certainly not outrageous vocabulary. I wrote it with you in mind!

If you are still in middle school, you are trying to learn how to study at precisely the right time. Sixth, seventh, and eighth grades—before that sometimes-cosmic leap to high school—are without a doubt when all these study skills should be mastered. If you're serious enough about studying to be reading this book, I doubt you'll have trouble with the concepts or the language.

A traditional college student (aged 18 to 25 or so) will have trouble making it to graduation without having learned all of the study techniques I cover, especially basic memory techniques. If you never found the time to learn them (and even if you know some tips but not every trick and gimmick covered in this book), I guarantee that truly mastering these memory techniques will help you long after you graduate (with As, of course!).

Parents reading this book are probably worried about their kid's grades, and they do have something to worry about—their child's school probably spends little, if any, time teaching basic study skills, which means those kids are not learning how to learn. And that means they are not learning how to succeed.

Don't for a minute underestimate the importance of your commitment to your child's success: Your involvement in your child's education is absolutely essential to his or her eventual success.

And you can help tremendously, even if you were not a great student yourself, even if you never learned great study skills. You can learn now with your child—not only will it help him or her in school, it will help you on the job, whatever your field.

The books in the *How to Study Program,* are meant to address all of these readers and their common problem—learning how to study so they can do better in school, or helping their kids to do so.

What Can Parents Do?

There are probably even more dedicated parents out there than dedicated students, since the first phone call at any of my radio or TV appearances comes from a sincere and worried parent asking, "What can I do to help my child do better in school?" Okay, here they are, the rules for parents of students of any age:

1. **Set up a homework area.** Free of distraction, well lit, with all necessary supplies handy.

2. **Set up a homework routine.** When and where it gets done. Studies have clearly shown that students who establish a regular routine are better organized and, as a result, more successful.

3. **Set homework priorities.** Actually, just make the point that homework is the priority—before a date, before TV, before going out to play, whatever.

4. **Make reading a habit**—for them, certainly, but also for you. Kids will inevitably do what you do, not what you say (even if you say not to do what you do).

5. **Turn off the TV.** Or at the very least, severely limit when and how much TV watching is appropriate. This may be the toughest suggestion to enforce. I know. I was once the parent of a teenager.

6. **Talk to the teachers.** Find out what your kids are supposed to be learning. If you don't know the books they're supposed to be reading, what's expected of them in class, and how much homework they should be scheduling, you can't really give them the help they need.

7. **Encourage and motivate,** but don't nag them to do their homework. It doesn't work. The more you insist, the quicker they will tune you out.

8. **Supervise their work,** but don't fall into the trap of doing their homework. Checking (i.e., proofreading) a paper, for example, is a positive way to help your child in school. But if you simply put in corrections without your child learning from her mistakes, you're not helping her at all...except in the belief that she is not responsible for her own work.

9. **Praise them when they succeed,** but don't overpraise them for mediocre work. Kids know when you're being insincere and, again, will quickly tune you out.

10. **Convince them of reality.** (This is for older students.) Okay, I'll admit it's almost as much of a stretch as turning off the TV, but learning and believing that the real world will not care about their grades, but will measure them by what they know and what they can do, is a lesson that will save many tears (probably yours). It's probably never too early to (carefully) let your boy or girl genius get the message that life is not fair.

11. **If you can afford it,** get your kid(s) a computer and all the software they can handle. There really is no avoiding it: Your kids, whatever their ages, absolutely must be computer-savvy in order to survive in and after school.

12. **Turn off the TV already!**

13. **Get wired.** The Internet is the greatest invention of our age and an unbelievable tool for students of any age. It is impossible for a student to succeed without the ability to surf online in this age of technology. They've got to be connected.

14. **But turn off IM (Instant Messaging) while doing homework.** They will attempt to convince you that they can write a term paper, do their geometry homework, and IM their friends at the same time. Parents who believe this have also been persuaded that the best study area is in front of the TV.

If You're Going Back to School Yourself

If you're going back to high school, college, or graduate school at age 25, 45, 65, or 85—you probably need the help my books offer more than anyone! Why? Because the longer you've been out of school, the more likely it is that you don't remember what you've forgotten. And you've probably forgotten what you're supposed to remember! As much as I emphasize that it's rarely too early to learn good study habits, I must also emphasize that it's never too late.

If you're returning to school and attempting to carry even a partial load of courses while simultaneously holding down a job, raising a family, or both, there are some particular problems you face that you probably didn't the first time you were in school:

Time and money pressures. When all you had to worry about was going to school, it was easier than going to school, raising a family, and working for a living simultaneously! Your organizational and memory skills will be tested daily.

Self-imposed fears of inadequacy. You may well convince yourself that you're just "out of practice" with all this school stuff. You don't even remember what to do with a highlighter! While some of this fear is valid, most is not. The valid part is that you are returning to an academic atmosphere, one that you may not have visited for a decade or two. And it is different (which I'll discuss more next) than the "work-a-day" world. That's just a matter of adjustment and—trust me—it will take a matter of days, if not hours, to dissipate. I suspect what many of you are really fearing is that you just aren't in that school "mentality" anymore, that you don't "think" the same way. Or, perhaps more pertinent to this book, that the skills you need to succeed in school are rusty.

I think these last fears are groundless. You've been out there thinking and doing for quite a few years, perhaps very success-fully, so it's really ridiculous to think school will be so different. It won't be. Relax. And while you may think your study skills are rusty, as we discussed earlier, you've probably been using them every day in your career. Even if I can't convince you, you have my *How to Study Program* as your refresher course. It will probably teach you more about studying than you ever forgot you knew.

Maybe you're worried because you didn't exactly light up the academic world the first time around. Well, neither did Edison or Einstein or a host of other successful people. But then, you've changed rather significantly since then, haven't you? Concen-trate on how much more qualified you are for school now than you were then!

Feeling you're "out of your element." This is a slightly dif-ferent fear, the fear that you just don't fit in anymore. After all, you're not 18 again. But then, neither are fully half the college students on campuses today. That's right: Fully 50 percent of all college students are older than 25. The reality is, you'll prob-ably feel more in your element now than you did the first time around!

You'll see teachers differently. Probably a plus. It's doubtful you'll have the same awe you did the first time around. At worst, you'll consider teachers your equals. At best, you'll consider them younger and not necessarily as successful or experienced as you are. In either event, you probably won't be quite as ready to treat your college professors as if they were minor deities.

There are differences in academic life. It's slower than the "real" world, and you may well be moving significantly faster than its normal pace. When you were 18, an afternoon without classes meant a game of Frisbee. Now it might mean catching up on a week's worth of errands, cooking (and freezing) a week's worth of dinners, and/or writing four reports due this week. Despite your own hectic schedule, do not expect campus life to accelerate in response. You will have to get used to people and systems with far less interest in speed.

Some Random Thoughts About Learning

Learning shouldn't be painful and certainly doesn't have to be boring, though it's far too often both. It's not necessarily going to be painless, either. Sometimes you actually have to work hard to figure something out or get a project done. That is reality.

It's also reality that everything isn't readily apparent or easily understandable. Learning something slowly doesn't mean there's something wrong with you. It may be a subject that virtually everybody learns slowly.

A good student doesn't panic when something doesn't seem to be getting through the haze. He just takes his time, follows whatever steps apply, and remains confident that the lightbulb will indeed inevitably go on.

Parents often ask me, "How can I motivate my teenager?" My initial response is usually to say, "If I knew the answer to that question, I would have retired very wealthy quite some time ago." However, I think there is an answer, but it's not something parents can do—it's something the student has to decide: Are you going to spend the school day interested and alert or bored and resentful?

It's really that simple. Since you have to go to school anyway, why not develop the attitude that you might as well be active and learn as much as possible instead of being miserable? The difference between a C and an A or B for many students is, I firmly believe, merely a matter of wanting to do better. As I constantly stress in radio and TV interviews, inevitably you will leave school. And very quickly, you'll discover the premium is on what you know and what you can do. Grades won't count anymore, and neither will tests. So you can learn it all now or regret it later.

How many times have you said to yourself, "I don't know why I'm bothering trying to learn this calculus, algebra, geometry, physics, chemistry, history, whatever. I'll never use this again!"? Unless you've got a patent on some great new fortune-telling device, you have no clue what you're going to need to know tomorrow or next week, let alone next year or in a decade.

I've been amazed in my own life how things I did with no specific purpose in mind (except probably to earn money or meet a girl) turned out years later to be not just invaluable to my life or career, but essential. How was I to know when I took German as my language elective in high school that the most important international trade show in book publishing was in Frankfurt, Germany? Or that the basic skills I learned one year working for an accountant (while I was writing my first book) would become essential when I later started four companies?

Or how important basic math skills would be in selling and negotiating over the years? (Okay, I'll admit it: I haven't used a differential equation in 30 years, but, hey, you never know!)

So learn it all. And don't be surprised if the subject you'd vote "least likely to ever be useful" winds up being the key to your fame and fortune.

There Aren't Many Study Rules

Though I immodestly maintain that my *How to Study Program* is the most helpful to the most people, there are certainly plenty of other purported study books out there. Inevitably, these books promote the authors' "system," which usually means what they did to get through school. This "system," whether basic and traditional or wildly quirky, may or may not work for you. So what do you do if "their" way of taking notes makes no sense to you? Or you master their highfalutin' "Super Student Study Symbols" and still get Cs?

There are very few "rights" and "wrongs" out there in the study world. There's certainly no single "right" way to attack a multiple choice test or take notes. So don't get fooled into thinking there is, especially if what you're doing seems to be working for you.

Needless to say, don't read my books looking for some single, inestimable system of "rules" that works for everyone. You won't find it, 'cause there's no such bird.

You will find a plethora of techniques, tips, tricks, gimmicks, and what-have-you, some or all of which may work for you, some of which won't. Pick and choose, change and adapt, figure out what works for you. Because you are the one responsible for creating your study system, not me.

I've used the phrase "Study smarter, not harder" as a sort of catch phrase in promotion and publicity for the *How to Study Program* for 20 years. So what does it mean to you? Does it mean I guarantee you'll spend less time studying? Or that the less studying you do, the better your grades will be? Or that studying isn't ever supposed to be difficult?

Hardly. It means that studying inefficiently is wasting time that could be spent doing other (okay, probably more fun) things and that getting your studying done as quickly and efficiently as possible is a realistic, worthy, and attainable goal. I'm no stranger to hard work, but I'm not a monastic dropout who thrives on self-flagellation. I try not to work harder than I have to!

What You'll Remember from This One

If you have trouble remembering your own phone number, this is the book for you. This new edition is even more complete— a simple, practical, easy-to-use memory book that will help you:

- Remember numbers.
- Remember dates and facts.
- Retain more of what you read the first time you read it.
- Take notes that will help you score well on tests.
- Remember numbers.
- Build a bigger vocabulary.
- Remember how to spell.
- Remember names and faces.
- Remember numbers. (And yes, I'm repeating this for emphasis because I get the feeling this is everyone's biggest problem!)

What's more, *Improve Your Memory* will help you do all of this without investing a mind-numbing amount of time and effort. Its advice is easy to learn and even easier to apply.

Along the way, you might even develop the skills for knowing at all times where you've left your glasses, car keys, or wallet.

The best way to approach this book is to read Chapters 1 through 9 straight through, then go back and review some of the mechanics of memory improvement contained in Chapters 3 through 9. If you have ADD—or are the parent of someone who does—be sure to read Chapter 10.

After this review, take the tests in Chapter 11 and see how much you've improved your memory. I'm sure you'll be amazed. When you've finished this book, you'll be effortlessly flexing mental muscles you never knew you had!

The Last Bit of Introductory Stuff

Before we get on with all the tips and techniques necessary to remember anything you need to, when you need to, let me make two important points about all my study books.

First, while I believe in gender equality, I find constructions such as "he and she," "s/he," "womyn," and other such stretches to be sometimes painfully awkward. I have therefore attempted to sprinkle pronouns of both genders throughout the text.

Second, you will find that many similar pieces of advice, examples, lists, phrases, and sections appear in several of my books. Certainly *How to Study*, which is an overview of all the study skills, necessarily contains, though in summarized form, some of each of the other five books.

The repetition is unavoidable. While I urge everyone to read all the books in the series, but especially *How to Study,* they are six individual books. And many people buy only one of them. Consequently, I must include in each book the pertinent material for that topic, even if that material is repeated in another book.

That said, I can guarantee that the nearly 1,000 pages of my *How to Study Program* contain the most wide-ranging, comprehensive, and complete system of studying ever published. I have attempted to create a system that is usable, useful, practical, and learnable. One that you can use—whatever your age, whatever your level of achievement, whatever your IQ—to start doing better in school, in work, and in life immediately.

Good luck.

Ron Fry

Chapter 1

Start Your Memory Banks

Which do you think you're more likely to remember—your first date with your future spouse (even if it was decades ago) or what you had for breakfast last Thursday?

Probably the former (though not if last Thursday was your first experiment with yak butter).

Which event conjures up the most memories—the Blizzard of 1996 or the last time it rained (unless, of course, it really poured cats and dogs)?

Which name would you find difficult to forget—Joe Smith or Irina Khakamada? We'll deal with how to remember spelling Ms. Khakamada in Chapters 5 and 7.

What do all the "memorable" names, dates, places, and events have in common? The fact that they're different. What makes something memorable is its extraordinariness—how much it differs from our normal experiences.

The reason so many of us forget where we put the car keys or our glasses is that putting these objects down is the most ordinary of occurrences, part and parcel of the most humdrum aspects of our lives. (Believe it or not, according to *Reader's Digest,* the average adult spends 16 hours a year trying to find his or her keys.) We have trouble remembering facts and formulas from books and classroom lectures for the same reason. To be schooled is to be bombarded with facts day in and day out. How do you make those facts memorable?

Beef Up Your RAM

In order to understand how to make the important facts memorable, how to keep them stored safely at least until final exams, let's first take a look at how the brain and, more specifically, memory work.

Think of your brain as a computer—an organic computer, wired with nerves, hooked up to various input devices (your five senses), and possessed of both ROM (read-only memory) and RAM (random-access memory).

The ROM is the permanent data you can't touch—the information that tells your heart to pump and your lungs to breathe.

On the other hand, RAM is much more accessible. Like most PCs, your brain stores RAM in two places: short-term memory (cache or virtual memory) and long-term memory (your hard drive).

Okay, so what happens to input in this system?

Let's Play Memory Tag

Given the bombardment of data we receive every day, our brains constantly are making choices. Data either goes in one ear and out the other, or it stops in short-term memory. But when the cache or vitural memory is overloaded, the brain is left with a choice—jettison some old information or pass it on to the hard drive.

How does it make a decision about which information to pass on and where to store it?

Well, scientists aren't positive about this yet, but, of course, they have theories.

The most readily stored and accessed is data that's been rehearsed—gone over again and again. Most of us readily access our knowledge of how to read, how to drive, the year Columbus "discovered" America, the name of the first president of the United States, and other basics without any difficulty at all. (At worst, you remember "Columbus sailed the ocean blue in 1492." And aren't we lucky he did? Otherwise, if only in the interests of historical accuracy, we'd have to remember something like "Leif Eriksson landed at L'Anse aus Meadows, Newfoundland, somewhere between 997 and 1003.") We've worn familiar paths through our memory banks accessing this type of information.

Why, then, can some people recite the names, symbols, and atomic weights of the elements of the periodic table—while they're playing (and winning) Trivial Pursuit—as easily as they can the date of Columbus's dubious achievement?

To return to our computer analogy, this information has been "tagged" or "coded" in some way so that it can be retrieved easily by the user. For instance, before storing a file in your computer's long-term RAM, you give it a name, one that succinctly describes its contents. In other words, you make the file stand out in some way from the host of other files you've stored on your disk drive.

For some people, myriad bits of data are almost automatically tagged so that they can quite easily and handily be stored and retrieved. But most of us, if we are to have exceptional memories, must make a special effort.

Can You Twist and Shout... And Remember?

First and foremost, there are three very different kinds of memory—visual, verbal, and kinesthetic, each of which can be strong or weak, and only the first two of which are associated with your brain. (This is, of course, a gross simplification of what we term "memory." Surveys have found more than a hundred different memory tasks in everyday life that can cause people problems, each of which require a different strategy! Sorry to break it to you, but just because you've learned an easy way to remember a 100-digit number [see Chapter 8] does not guarantee that you won't spend days looking for those darned glasses.)

Most people have the easiest time strengthening their visual memories, which is why so many memory techniques involve forming "mental pictures."

To strengthen our verbal memories, we use rhymes, songs, letter substitutions, and other mnemonic gimmicks.

Finally, don't underestimate the importance of kinesthetic memory, or what your body remembers. Athletes and dancers certainly don't have to be convinced that the muscles, joints, and tendons of their bodies seem to have their own memories. Neither does anyone who's ever remembered a phone number by moving his fingers and "remembering" how it's dialed.

The next time you have to remember a list, any list, say each item out loud and move some part of your body at the same time. A dancer can do the time step and remember her history lecture. A baseball pitcher can associate each movement of his windup with another item in a list he has to memorize. Even random body movements will do. For example, if you have to memorize a list of countries, just associate each one with a specific movement. For Burundi, lift your right index finger while saying it. For Zimbabwe, rotate your neck. Bend a knee for Equador and raise your left hand for San Marino. Kick Latvia in the shins and twirl your hair for Kampuchea. When you have to remember this list of countries, just start moving! It may look a little strange—especially if you make your movements a little too exotic or dramatic in the middle of geography class—but if it works better than anything else for you, who cares?

You can also use this newfound memory as a backup to your brain. While you may still memorize key phone numbers, for example, you may also accompany each recitation with the hand movements necessary to actually dial the number. You'll probably find that even if you forget the "mental" tricks you used, your "body memory" will run (or lift or squat or bend or shake) to the rescue!

Once You Learn the Tricks...

Students, of course, must possess or develop good memories, or they risk mediocrity or failure. The mere act of getting by in school means remembering a lot of dates, mathematical and scientific formulas, historical events, characters and plots, and sometimes entire poems. (I had a biology teacher who made us memorize the 52 parts of a frog's body. All of which, of course, have been absolutely essential to my subsequent career success. Just kidding.)

Practically, there are two ways of going about this. The most familiar way is rehearsal or repetition. By any name, it is the process of reading or pronouncing something over and over until you've learned it "by heart."

But a much easier way—getting back to our computer analogy—is to tag or code things we are trying to remember and to do so with images and words that are either outrageous or very familiar.

For instance, have you ever wondered how, in the days before index cards, ballpoint pens, or teleprompters, troubadours memorized song cycles and politicians memorized lengthy speeches? Well, in the case of the great Roman orator Cicero, it was a matter of associating the parts of his speeches with the most familiar objects in his life—the rooms of his home. Perhaps the opening of a speech would be linked to his bedroom, the next part to his yard. As he progressed through the speech, he would, in essence, mentally take his usual morning stroll, passing through the rooms of his home.

This simple method works very well for a relatively short, related list, such as what you need at the grocery store. You can use the rooms in your house, the items in a particular room, even the route you drive to work. Use the landmarks you see every day to remind you of various items you need to buy at the store: Start right in the garage—remember the garbage bags! Turn the key—that's right, the broccoli. As you pass the dry cleaner's, picture soap suds spilling out the door (laundry detergent); McDonald's should remind you to pick up the hamburger meat (and, hopefully, the buns and ketchup!); picture a roll of paper towels hanging off that traffic light. Turn on your windshield wipers. Oh, yeah, the French bread! Oops, and the bananas. If you're going to use landmarks to remember lists, write down those you're going to use beforehand. That way, you won't get mixed up by others you notice along your route.

Why limit your list? Well, unless you live in a 35-room mansion or drive three hours to work, there are only so many rooms and landmarks you can easily use!

In other cases, more outrageous associations work much better. The more ridiculous or impossible the association, the more memorable it is. Although absentmindedness is not one of the problems we will try to solve in this book, a common cure for it illustrates my point.

If you frequently have trouble remembering, say, where you put down your pen, get into the habit of conjuring up some startling image linking (a key word later on in this book) the pen and the place. For example, as you're putting your pen down on the kitchen table, think about eating peas off a plate with it or of the pen sticking straight up in a pile of mashed potatoes. Even days later, when you think, "Hmm, where did I leave that pen?" the peas and plate (or mashed potatoes) will come to mind, reminding you of the kitchen table.

...The Rest Is Easy

These are the essential principles of memory for which the computer analogy is particularly apt. After all, when dealing with the mind, as with the machine, the GIGO (garbage in, garbage out) rule applies. If you passively allow your brain's processes to decide what and how items are stored, you will have a jumbled memory from which it is difficult to extract even essential bits of knowledge.

On the other hand, if you are selective and careful about assigning useful tags to the items headed for the long-term memory banks, you are on the way to being able to memorize the Manhattan telephone directory!

CHAPTER 2

AND NOW
FOR A LITTLE QUIZ

I know what you're thinking. You bought this book so you could improve your memory and perform better on exams and those darned pop quizzes, and now I turn around and throw some more tests your way. I could note that "Them's the breaks!"

Or, as one of my high school teachers used to say, I could encourage you to think of tests as your best friends (no, it wasn't the crazy biology teacher I told you about in Chapter 1). In this book, and throughout your academic career, tests will give you the measure of how far you've come…and how far you've got to go. Follow the advice in this book and your score on similar tests in the last chapter should be 25 percent higher.

Test 1: Numbers

Look at the number directly below this paragraph for no more than 10 seconds. Then cover the page (or, better yet, close the book and put it aside) and write down as much of it—in order—as you can.

674216899411539273

Test 2: Words and Definitions

Below are 15 obscure words along with their definitions. Study this list for 60 seconds. Then cover it up and take the test following the list. Allow yourself no more than 90 seconds to complete the quiz...and no peeking.

Harmattan	A dry, parching land breeze
Doggo	Concealed, out of sight
Ihram	Dress worn by male Muslims on pilgrimage to Mecca
Iiwi	A Hawaiian honeycreeper with a red body, black wings, and very curved red bill
Posticum	Back part of a building
Tamandua	A tree-dwelling anteater
Jinker	An Australian sulky (cart)
Millilux	A unit of illumination
Elision	The omission of a vowel, consonant, or syllable in pronunciation
Caudate	Having a tail
Dolor	Sorrow
Ordure	Excrement
Ubisunt	A poetic motif
Tussah	A tan silk from India
Squamous	Covered with scales

Have you studied the words diligently? Okay, no cheating now, fill in the blanks:

1. _____ is a dress worn by male Muslims on pilgrimage to Mecca.

2. Monkeys would be considered _____.

3. Writing poetry might involve the use of a _____.

4. Most lizards are _____.

5. If you're an ant, you would avoid a _____.

6. Playing hide and seek, John was really _____.

7. If you visit the Sahara, you'll undoubtedly experience a _____.

8. An _____ is a Hawaiian honeycreeper with a red body, black wings, and very curved red bill.

9. In Bollywood movies, the female star might wear a _____.

10. Using _____ might help your roses bloom.

11. "Back off, buddy, and don't give me any _____."

12. "Meet me around the corner by the _____."

13. "What, are you trying to save a _____? Turn that light up!"

14. The meteorological stations of Alaska are part of a single _____.

15. "Hey, mate, bring that _____ around."

Test 3: Names

Take three minutes to memorize the names of the following directors and their films (all Oscar winners for Best Picture, by the way):

Rocky	John G. Avildsen
Chicago	Rob Marshall
Kramer vs. Kramer	Robert Benton
Midnight Cowboy	John Schlesinger
Amadeus	Milos Forman
Driving Ms. Daisy	Bruce Beresford
The English Patient	Anthony Minghella
American Beauty	Sam Mendes
The Deer Hunter	Michael Cimino
A Beautiful Mind	Ron Howard
Dances with Wolves	Kevin Costner
Platoon	Oliver Stone
Ordinary People	Robert Redford
The French Connection	William Friedkin
The Last Emperor	Bernardo Bertolucci

Time's up! Okay, cover the list and fill in as many of the blanks as you can. If you get last names only, that's fine. Take another three minutes to complete the quiz:

1. The *French Connection:* _____

2. Michael Cimino: _____

3. Milos Forman: _____

4. *Rocky:* _____

5. Robert Redford: _____

6. *Platoon:* _____

7. Ron Howard: _____

8. *The Last Emperor:* _____

9. Sam Mendes: _____

10. *Chicago:* _____

11. John Schlesinger: _____

12. *Dances with Wolves:* _____

13. Anthony Minghella: _____

14. *Driving Ms. Daisy:* _____

15. Robert Benton: _____

Test 4: Dates

Here are the dates of 15 historical events. Take up to three minutes to memorize them, then cover the page and take the quiz that follows.

1865   The tallest mountain in the world is named after Sir George Everest, the British Surgeon General.

1588   Defeat of the Spanish Armada.

1762   Catherine the Great becomes Czarina of Russia.

1819   Spain cedes Florida to the U.S.

1620   The Plymouth Colony is founded and the Mayflower Compact signed.

1871   The worst forest fire in U.S. history destroys almost 4 million acres.

1797   John Adams inaugurated as the second U.S. President.

1918   The Bolsheviks kill the Czar.

2004   Mikhail Fradkov named prime minister of the Russian Federation.

1556   Akbar named Mogul Emperor of India.

1765   James Watt invents the steam engine.

1803   The Marbury vs. Madison decision, in which the Supreme Court gives itself the power to declare acts of Congress unconstitutional.

1682   Pennsylvania is founded.

1799   The Rosetta Stone is discovered in Egypt.

1605   Cervantes publishes *Don Quixote de la Mancha.*

1. Nearly ____ million acres were destroyed in _____ during the worst fire in U.S. history.

2. _____ invented the _____ in _____.

3. _____, the second President of the United States, was inaugurated in _____.

4. The _____ was signed in the state of _____ in _____.

5. In _____, the _____ was defeated by _____.

6. _____ was named prime minister of _____ in _____.

7. The state of _____ was founded in _____ by _____.

8. In _____, the _____ decision gave the Supreme Court the power to _____.

9. In _____, the _____ was discovered in _____.

10. _____ was named Mogul emperor of _____ in _____.

11. _____ gave his name to _____ in _____.

12. _____, written by _____, was published in _____.

13. _____ became _____ of Russia in _____.

14. The _____ killed the czar in _____.

15. The state of _____ was ceded to the U.S. by _____ in _____.

Test 5: Reading Retention

Read the following excerpt from *The Natural Woman's Guide to Hormone Replacement Therapy* by M. Sara Rosenthal (New Page Books, 2003), then answer the questions following. Give yourself two minutes to read the text and two minutes to answer the questions without referring back to the paragraph.

In July 2001, a study by the U.S. National Heart, Lung, and Blood Institute, part of a huge research program called the Women's Health Initiative (WHI), suggested that Hormone Replacement Therapy (HRT) should not be recommended for long-term use. In fact, the results were so alarming, the study was halted before its completion date. It was found that Prempro, a combination of estrogen and progestin, which was a "standard issue" HRT formulation for postmenopausal women, increased the risk of invasive breast cancer, heart disease, stroke, and pulmonary embolisms (blood clots). However, Prempro did reduce the incidence of bone fractures from osteoporosis and colon cancer. Nevertheless, the idea that HRT is a long-term "fountain of youth" is slowly dissolving. The study participants were informed in a letter that they should stop taking their pills. HRT, used in the short-term to relieve menopausal symptoms, is still considered a good option, and there was no evidence to suggest that short-term use of HRT was harmful. The study only has implications for women on HRT for long-term use—something that was recommended to millions of women during the past 20 years because of perceived protection against heart disease.

In 1998, an earlier trial, known as the Heart and Estrogen/Progestin Replacement Study (HERS), looked at whether HRT was reduced in women who already had heart disease. HRT was not found to have any beneficial effect. Women who were at risk for breast cancer were never advised to go on HRT; similarly, women who had suffered a stroke or considered at risk for blood clots were also never considered good candidates for HRT. It had long been known that breast cancer was a risk of long-term HRT, as well as stroke and blood clots. However, many women made the HRT decision based on the fact that it was long believed to protect women from heart disease. Millions of women are now questioning whether they should be on HRT in light of these facts and findings.

Today, the only thing the "experts" can agree on is that the HRT decision is highly individual and must be an informed decision, where all of the possible risks and benefits of taking—or not taking—HRT are disclosed. Women with a family history of breast cancer were never considered good HRT candidates. So, for this group of women, things have not changed. However, women who were considered at higher risk for heart disease due to family history or other risk factors, such as Type 2 diabetes, are now more confused than ever.

Questions

1. The most descriptive title for this excerpt would be:
   A. HRT—no long-term "fountain of youth"
   B. Uses and abuses of Prempro
   C. The HERS Study
   D. New implications of long-term use of HRT

2. Women were never good candidates for HRT if they:
   A. Were overweight
   B. Had suffered a stroke
   C. Were at risk of breast cancer
   D. Were underweight

3. The WHI study concluded that:
   A. Women with Type 2 diabetes should not drink alcohol.
   B. Breast cancer rates are rising.
   C. HRT should not be recommended for long-term use.
   D. HRT is a short-term "fountain of youth."

4. Prempro is a combination of:
   A. Estrogen and a placebo
   B. Estrogen and progestin
   C. Progestin and aspirin
   D. Aspirin and estrogen

5. HRT has been recommended for the past 20 years because it was thought to protect women against:

A. Breast cancer

B. Uterine cancer

C. Heart disease

D. Stroke

Here's another chance to test your memory with information that may be pertinent to those of you on your way to business school, excerpted from *Your MBA Game Plan* by Omari Bouknight and Scott Shrum (Career Press, 2003):

In many ways, consultants are made for business school. As a consultant, you most likely have a strong academic background, have had multiple experiences with myriad companies, and have finely tuned analytical and interpersonal skills. Additionally, you have direct access to a cadre of b-school graduates through your firm, who serve as great advisors.

Unfortunately, more applicants fall into the consultant category than probably any other profile type. As a result, it is also probably more difficult to differentiate yourself as a consultant. Consulting firms often have standardized analyst programs that "feed" business schools with applicants after they've had two or three years of experience. Over time, many b-schools have become somewhat wary of these programs, because of their tendency to produce applicants who are simply looking to "get their ticket punched."

You can avoid the perception that you're just trying to get your ticket punched by being explicit about how you intend to utilize an MBA to reach your career goals. That's not to say that you shouldn't express an interest in returning to consulting. But if you do go down that path, you need to make sure to discuss how you see yourself having an impact on the organization. Do you see an opportunity to increase your clients' revenues through Customer Relationship Management? Then discuss how you want to capitalize on this opportunity by studying the intersection of marketing and technology. The bottom line is that you have to provide tangible reasons for wanting to attend b-school. In many ways, if you intend to return to consulting, this is even more important than if you're planning on switching careers.

Along the lines of being explicit in your writing, try your best not to introduce consultant jargon into your essays and interviews. Consultants have a tendency to write essays that are high-level and ambiguous. Admissions counselors comment that consultants often fail to adequately explain their specific actions on projects and the results of those actions. To the extent that you can quantify both, you will stand out from the pack.

The average number of years of work experience at top business schools approaches five. Consultants, however, tend to apply to schools after only two to four years of experience. If you fall into this group, then you should expect to be questioned about it and should find ways to emphasize your maturity. One way to do that is by discussing activities in which you are involved outside of consulting. Because of the long hours associated with their profession, many applicants from consulting are unable to talk about anything that is unrelated to work. To the extent that you are able to weave activities outside of the consulting world into your story, you will be able to differentiate yourself.

Questions

6. Consultant jargon:

   A. Will impress an interviewer.

   B. May be used in essays but should be avoided in interviews.

   C. May be used in interviews but should be avoided in essays.

   D. Should never be used at all.

7. The average numbers of years of work experience at top business schools is:

   A. Four

   B. Ten

   C. Five

   D. None

8. The most prevalent category of experience for business school applicants is:

   A. Consultant

   B. Student

   C. Trader

   D. Stock broker

9. When you graduate from business school, your degree is:

A. Masters of Business

B. Bachelor of Business Arts

C. Masters of Business Administration

D. Masters

10. If you intend to return to consulting after business school, you should:

A. Never admit it.

B. Make a point of emphasizing your plan.

C. Rethink your life goals.

D. Provide tangible reasons for attending business school.

To check how you did in this last test section, see the answers at the end of the chapter. Go back and check the book itself to figure out the answers to the others.

How did you do?

Take a piece of paper and write down the scores you got on each of these exercises. This will indicate how much improvement you need to successfully recall the material you learn in school. It will also provide a benchmark so that you can see how far you've come when you take similar quizzes in the last chapter.

The emphasis of these tests was not arbitrary. It corresponds exactly with the skills you will be learning throughout this book: memorizing chains of information (such as the film/director and the date/event pairings), developing a sense for numbers, remembering what you read, and getting a better grasp on vocabulary.

By the way, I realize that the text for Test 4 did not mention that Pennsylvania was founded by William Penn, that the British Navy destroyed the Spanish Armada, or that the Mayflower landed in what was soon called Massachusetts. Shouldn't you already know these facts? You get my point.

Answers to Test 5: **1.** D, **2.** B, **3.** C, **4.** B, **5.** C, **6.** D, **7.** C, **8.** A, **9.** C, **10.** D.

CHAPTER 3

ROY G. BIV AND FRIENDS

C hapter 1 addressed the need to establish tags or codes for items we wish to remember so that our minds will have relatively little difficulty retrieving them from long-term memory.

In this chapter, we will begin talking about one of the methods used for "tagging" items before they enter that morass of memory.

The "chain link" method will help you remember items that appear in sequence, whether it's the association of a date with an event, a scientific term with its meaning, or other facts or objects that are supposed to "go together."

The basis for the chain-link system is that memory works best when you associate the unfamiliar with the familiar, though sometimes the association may be very odd. But to really make it effective, the odder the better.

Our Boy Roy

One of the simplest methods is to try to remember just the first letter of a sequence. That's how "Roy G. Biv" (the colors of the spectrum, in order from left to right—red, orange, yellow, green, blue, indigo, violet) got famous. Or "Every Good Boy Does Fine," to remember the notes on a musical staff. Or, perhaps the simplest of all, "FACE," to remember the notes in between. (The latter two use words to remember letters.)

Of course, not many sequences work out as nicely as HOMES, an effective way to remember the Great Lakes (Huron, Ontario, Michigan, Erie, and Superior). If you tried to memorize the signs of the zodiac with this method, you'd wind up with (A)ries, (T)aurus, (G)emini, (C)ancer, (L)eo, (V)irgo, (L)ibra, (S)corpio, (S)agittarius, (C)apricorn, (A)quarius, (P)isces. Now maybe you can make a name or a place or something out of ATGCLVLSSCAP, but I can't!

One solution is to make up a simple sentence that uses the first letters of the list you're trying to remember as the first letters of each word. For example, "A Tall Giraffe Chewed Leaves Very Low, Some Slow Cows At Play."

Wait a minute! It's the same number of words as the zodiacal signs themselves. Why not just figure out some way to memorize the Zodiac? What's better about the second set? A couple of things. First of all, it's easier to picture the giraffe and cow and what they're doing. As we'll soon see, creating such mental images is a very powerful way to remember almost anything. Second, because the words in our sentence bear some relationship to each other, they're much easier to remember. Go ahead, try it. See how long it takes you to memorize the sentence versus all the signs.

Remember: Make your sentence(s) memorable to you. Any sentence or series of words that helps you remember these letters will do. Here are just two more I created in a few seconds: A Tall Girl Called Lively Vera Loved to Sip Sodas from Cans And Plates. Any Tiny Gerbil Could Love Venus. Long Silly Snakes Could All Pray. Isn't it easy to make up silly, memorable pictures in your head for these?

There is a limit to this technique: Unless the list itself is familiar to you (like the colors of the spectrum), this method will do you little good. For example, medical students for decades have used the mnemonic On Old Olympia's Towering Top A Finn And German Vault And Hop to remember the list of cranial nerves (olfactory, optic, oculomotor, trochlear, trigeminal, abducens, facial, auditory, glossopharyngeal, vagus, accessory, and hypoglossal). The only way the letter "G" in "German" is going to remind you of "glossopharyngeal" is if you have already spent a significant amount of time studying (memorizing?) this list!

The Rain in Spain

Let's say that I was a history major who wanted to remember the year President Nixon resigned, which was 1974.

The usual way for me to do this would be to repeat "Nixon, resignation, 1974, Nixon, resignation, 1974..." ad nauseum. How much easier would it be to just say "Nixon walked out the door in '74!" I've established a link between Nixon's resignation (him walking out the door—and out of the presidency) and 1974, the date he resigned. (You'll learn more about how to remember dates in Chapter 8.)

In addition, I was able to use another terrific memory technique—rhyming. Rhyme schemes, no matter how silly or banal, can help us remember things for years. For instance, who can forget that it's "i before e except after c, or when it sounds like a as in neighbor and weigh"?

The Stranger the Better

Let's step away from schoolwork for a moment to consider the case of a woman who can't remember where she puts anything—car keys, glasses, purse...

Using the chain-link method would ensure that she would never forget. For instance, let's say she puts her car keys down on her kitchen counter and, as she does, thinks of a car plowing right into the kitchen and through the countertop. Will that woman be able to forget what she did with her keys? Would you?

Or, to pick an example more germane to academic life, let's say that you wanted to remember that mitosis is the process whereby one cell divides itself into two. Instead of repeating word and definition countless times, why not think, "My toes is dividing," and form a mental picture of two of your toes separating? Much easier, isn't it?

To make life even easier for those of you forever forgetting your keys, make it a habit to simply put them in the same place every time—in a particular corner of the table, on a hook, wherever—and never, ever deviate. It will be one less thing to remember (and, if you believe *Reader's Digest*, save you 16 hours a year).

Show Me...Missouri!

The best way to teach this technique is by example, so let's take another one. Suppose you wanted to remember the following list of a dozen U.S. states and their nicknames:

New Jersey	Garden
Alabama	Yellowhammer
Texas	Lone Star
Indiana	Hoosier
New York	Empire
California	Golden
Missouri	Show Me
Connecticut	Nutmeg
Montana	Treasure
Georgia	Peach
Kentucky	Bluegrass
Louisiana	Pelican

Study the list for no more than two minutes, cover up the page, and try to write down as many combinations as you remember. Heck, you don't even have to do them in order—but you get serious extra credit if you do!

How did you do? Did you get them all right? How long do you think you'd have to study this list to be able to recite it perfectly? I guarantee you it would take a lot less time if you established a chain link that you could just reel in out of your memory bank.

Here's how I would remember this list (and remember, make your pictures, associations, and stories memorable to you!):

I'm standing in a GARDEN wearing my NEW YELLOW JERSEY and holding a HAMMER, talking to my friends ALI BABA and TEX, who's been LONELY since his girlfriend STAR left him. "HOOSIER friend?" he asked me. "An INDIAN wearing a NEW EMPIRE dress." "CALIFORNIA? (Can I phone you?)" he asked her. "If you SHOW ME some GOLD," the little MISS replied sOURly.

I CONNECTED with my Jamaican friend, NUTMEG, MON, sporting a wicked TAN, who'd found some buried TREASURE. He was eating a GEORGIA PEACH while lying on the KENTUCKY BLUE GRASS. A PELICAN dive bombed him when he turned on LOUIE, LOUIE.

If you wanted, you could try to use the method we discussed earlier, making up a nonsense sentence or two using the first letters of each word (N, J, G, A, Y, T, L, S, I, H, N, Y, E, C, G, M, S, M, C, N, M, T, G, P, K, B, L, P). Here's my try: Now, Jimmy George, After You Toss Lori Sue Into Her Nice Yellow Ermine Coat, Get Ma Some Marshmallow Chocolate Nut Mints To Give Pa Kent Before Lori Pouts.

Is This Efficient?

You're probably wondering just how much time it took me to construct these ridiculous associations and the even more bizarre story to go with them. The answer: about three minutes (about the same for the sentence). I'll bet it will take you a lot longer to memorize the list of states and nicknames. And my way of doing this is so much more fun! Not only that, but I'd be willing to bet that you'll remember ' "California?" he asked her. "If you show me some gold," the little miss replied sourly.' a lot longer than the fact that California is the Golden State and Missouri the Show Me State.

The reason is that you use so much more of your brain when you employ techniques like this. Reciting a list of facts over and over to yourself uses only three of your faculties—sight (as you read them from the page), speech, and hearing—in carving the memory trail. Constructing a visual story like the one we just did also puts to work your imagination, perhaps the most powerful of your mind's many powers.

Those Were the Days...

Let's try another example—some legendary (but not exactly well-known) British Kings: Pir, Brutus, Maddan, Leir, Rivallo, Ferrex, Porrex, Danius, Ingenius, Cap, Geta, Severus, Coel, Runo.

Here's the way I would remember these monarchs:

I'm standing on a *pier* with my friends *Brutus* (in a toga) and John *Madden*, who's *leering* (picture those eyes!) at a dish full of *Rival* dog food. But it's a *ferret* eating the food, which looks like *porridge*. Just then, the *ingenious* *Danny Kaye*, wearing *several* colorful *caps*, *gets a cold* and *runs* away.

Remember, it's not enough to memorize this kind of story and use the words as triggers for your memory. You must create the picture in your mind using people and places you find meaningful. I have a hard time getting the picture of an animated John Madden out of my mind during football season, I'm a huge Danny Kaye fan, and my dog eats Rival. So this story clearly is easy for me to remember.

Now you try. How would you remember another obscure list— two dozen more British kings? (Didn't know there were so many, did you?)

Octavius, Constantius, Sulgenius, Eliud, Redon, Eldol, Heli, Lud, Penessil, Idvallo, Millus, Archgallo, Jago, Belinus, Rud Hud Hudibras, Gorboduc, Kimarcus, Trahern, Malgo, Keredic, Cadvan, Cadwallo, Vortimer, and Uther Pendragon.

Time yourself. When you can construct a series of pictures to remember a list like this—and remember it for a while, not just a day—all in less than five minutes, you are well on your way to mastering this powerful memory technique.

Hear My Song

Observations of people who have been in accidents or suffered other types of severe brain trauma have yielded many interesting insights into the ways our minds and memories work. For instance, people who have had the left side of their brains damaged might lose their ability to speak and remember words and facts, but often are still able to sing songs perfectly.

Current thinking on this is that the faculty for speech resides in the left hemisphere of the brain, while the ability to sing can be found in the right.

Since it is my feeling that the more of your mind's power you put behind the job of remembering, the better you'll do, I'd like to suggest song as another great way to remember strings of information.

For instance, I remember few things from high school chemistry (not having had memory training at that time). But one thing I'll never forget is that ionization is a dissociative reaction—the result of electrons becoming separated from their nuclei.

The reason I remember this is that Mr. Scott, my chemistry teacher, came into class singing (to the main theme from the opera *Grenada*) "I-, I-, I-onization. I-, I-, I-onization. Oh, this is, oh, this is a dissociative reaction in chemistry."

And there's the case of one of Robert Frost's most loved poems, "Stopping by Woods on a Snowy Evening." Did you ever realize that you could sing the entire poem to the music of "Hernando's Hideaway" by Xavier Cugat?

Try it with the last four lines—"The woods are lovely dark and deep, but I have promises to keep, and miles to go before I sleep. And miles to go before I sleep." Trust me: It works for the whole poem.

Music is one of the ways that you can create a chain link to improve your memory. As the examples we've already discussed show, there are many others:

Unusual. To the extent possible, make the chain-link scenarios you construct highly unusual.

Active. Don't think of an object just sitting there. Have it do something! Remember the woman with the car smashing through the kitchen counter earlier in the chapter? How can such an image be forgotten?

Emotional. Conjure up a scenario in establishing your chain link that elicits an emotional reaction—joy, sorrow, physical pain, whatever.

Rhyming. Many lessons for preschoolers and those in first and second grades are done with rhymes. If it works for them, it should work for you, right?

Acronyms. If you've taken trigonometry, you've probably come across good old Chief SOH-CAH-TOA. If you've been lucky enough to evade trig (or didn't have Mr. Oldehoff in seventh grade), you've missed one of the easiest way to remember trigonometric functions: Sine equals Opposite/ Hypotenuse; Cosine equals Adjacent/ Hypotenuse; Tangent equals Opposite/Adjacent.

Relax and Have Fun

You're probably thinking that all of this doesn't sound like it will make your life any easier. I know it seems like a lot of work to think of soundalikes, associations, and pictures and construct crazy scenarios or songs using them. Trust me: If you start applying these tips routinely, they will quickly become second nature and make you a more efficient student.

There's the Rub

The only problem with this method is that you might occasionally have trouble remembering what your soundalike signified in the first place. But the process of forming the link will usually obviate the problem, because the link to the original item is made stronger by the act of forming these crazy associations. Again, the crazier they are, the more memorable they are.

In the next chapter, we'll get away from straight factual memory for a little while and talk about how we can get a better grasp of material as we read through it the first time.

CHAPTER 4

READING AND REMEMBERING

Nothing you do as you pursue your studies in any subject will serve you as well as learning to read—and remembering what you've read whenever you need to. The ability to recall a great amount of detail without having to review is a tremendous benefit to any student.

In college, where the reading demands of a single course can be voluminous, just think how much more you could get out of your texts and how much more efficiently you could prepare for exams and term papers if you got most of the information you needed the first time around!

This chapter will show you how to do it…easily.

Reading to Remember

The best way to begin any reading assignment is to skim the pages to get an overall view of what information is included in the text. Then, read the text in detail and highlight it or take notes in your notebook.

I'm going to digress for a moment, taking your side to criticize a large number, perhaps even the majority, of the texts you're forced to plow through. This criticism is constructive: I want to show you the deficiencies in textbooks that you will have to overcome in order to be the best student you can be without unnecessary effort.

Think of the differences in writing and presentation between newspapers and textbooks. Newspapers are edited and designed to make reading simple. Most newspaper articles are organized using the "pyramid" approach: The first paragraph (the top of the pyramid) makes the major point of the story, then successive paragraphs add more detail and make related points, filling out the pyramid. You can get a pretty good handle on the day's news by reading the headlines and the first few paragraphs of each story. If you're interested in more details, just read on.

Textbooks, on the other hand, usually are not written to allow for such an approach. Many times authors begin with a relatively general introduction to the material, and then lead readers through their reasoning to major points.

The next time you have to read a history, geography, or similar text, try skimming the assigned pages first. Read the heads, subheads, and callouts, those brief notes or headings in the outside margins of each page that summarize the topic covered in the section. Read the first sentence of each paragraph. Then go back and read the details.

To summarize the skimming process:

1. If there is a title or heading, rephrase it as a question. This will be your purpose for reading.

2. Examine all the subheadings, illustrations, and graphics, as these will help you identify the significant matter within the text.

3. Read thoroughly the introductory paragraphs, the summary, and any questions at the chapter's end.

4. Read the first sentence of every paragraph—this is generally where the main idea is found.

5. Evaluate what you have gained from this process: Can you answer the questions at the end of the chapter? Could you intelligently participate in a class discussion of the material?

6. Write a brief summary that encapsulates what you have learned from your skimming.

7. Based on this evaluation, decide whether a more thorough reading is required.

I've found that this is the most effective way to preread a textbook. By the time I get to the material for which I am reading the chapter, my antennae are up and my mind is ready to soak up everything.

What if, despite your best efforts and my best advice, you simply cannot slog through another chapter? You simply can't fathom what the author is talking about? It may not be your fault. You will undoubtedly be assigned at least one textbook during your school life that is so obtuse you aren't sure whether to read it front to back, upside down, or inside out.

Don't keep wasting your time. Go to the library or bookstore and find another book that covers the same subject area, one that you can understand. (Your teacher or professor may even be able to recommend an alternative text—unless, of course, he or she wrote the unintelligible one, something that's not uncommon at the college level.) As long as both books cover relatively the same ground, you will save yourself a lot of time, energy, and frustration by substituting one for the other.

Reading Faster Without Speed Reading

While the heads, subheads, first sentences, and other author-provided hints will help you get a quick read on what a chapter's about, some of the words in that chapter will help you concentrate on the important points and ignore the unimportant. Knowing when to speed up, slow down, ignore, or really concentrate will help you read both faster and more effectively.

When you see words such as "likewise," "moreover," "also," "furthermore," and the like, you should know nothing new is being introduced. If you already know what's going on, speed up or skip what's coming entirely.

On the other hand, when you see words such as "on the other hand," "nevertheless," "however," "rather," "but," and their ilk, it's time to slow down—you're getting information that certainly adds a new perspective, and it may even contradict what you've just read.

Watch out for "payoff" words such as "in conclusion," "therefore," "thus," "consequently," "to summarize"—especially if you only have time to hit the high points of a chapter or if you're reviewing for a test. Here's where the real meat is, where everything that went before is happily tied up in a nice fat bow, a present that enables you to avoid having to unwrap the entire chapter.

One Chapter at a Time

Sometimes students have a desire to rush through the reading of textbooks to "get it over with." Granted, there are textbook writers who seem to go out of their way to encourage such a reaction. Don't fall into the trap.

Instead, before getting to the next chapter as rapidly as possible, stop to perform the following exercise:

- Write down definitions of any key terms you think are essential to understanding the topic.

- Write down questions and answers that you think help clarify the topic. Play teacher for a minute and design a pop quiz on the chapter.

- Write questions for which you don't have the answers, then go back and find them by rereading the chapter, noting questions you'd like to ask the professor or answer through further reading.

When Reading Is a Formula

Texts for mathematics, economics, and science require a slightly different treatment. You should follow the steps just outlined, but with one important addition: Make sure that you thoroughly understand the concepts expressed in the various charts and graphs, and do not move on to the next section unless you have mastered the previous one.

You must understand one section before moving on to the next, since the next concept is usually based on the previous one. If there are sample problems, solve those that tie in with the section you have just read to make sure that you understand the concepts imparted. If you still fail to grasp a key concept or equation, start again and try again. But don't move on—you'll just be wasting your time.

These texts require such a slow, steady approach, even one with a lot of backtracking or, for that matter, a lot of wrong turns. "Trial and error" is an accepted method of scientific research. The key, though, is to make it informed trial and error—having a clear idea of where you're heading and learning from each error. While trial and error is okay, it is much more important to be able to easily apply the same analysis (solution, reasoning) to a slightly different problem, which requires real understanding. Getting the right answer just because you eliminated every wrong one may be a very viable strategy for taking a test, but it's a lousy way to assure yourself you've actually learned something.

Understanding is especially essential in any technical subject. It's easy for some of you to do well on math tests because you have a great memory, are lucky, or have an innate math "sense." Trust me—sooner or later your luck runs out, your memory overloads, and your calculations stop making sense. You will reach a point where, without understanding, you will be left confused on the shore, watching your colleagues sail heroically to the promised land.

Whether math and science come easily to you or make you want to find the nearest pencil-pocketed computer nerd and throttle him, there are some ways you can do better at such technical subjects, without the world's greatest memory, a lot of luck, or any "radar":

- Whenever you can, "translate" numbers and formulae into words. To test your understanding, try to put your translation into different words.

- Even if you're not particularly visual, pictures can often help. You should try translating a particularly vexing math problem into a drawing or diagram.

- Before you even get down to solving a problem, is there any way for you to estimate the answer or, at least, to estimate the range within which the answer should fall (greater than one, but less than 10)? This is the easy way to at least make sure you wind up in the right ballpark.

- Play around. There are often different paths to the same solution or even equally valid solutions. If you find one, try to find others. This is a great way to increase your understanding of all the principles involved.

- When you are checking your calculations, try working backwards. I've found it to be an easier way to catch simple mathematical errors.

- Try to figure out what is being asked, what principles are involved, what information is important, and what is not. I can't resist an example here: A 45-rpm record is 6.57 inches in diameter. The label is two inches wide. The song lasts for exactly 3 minutes, 14 seconds. The record is .012 inches thick.

  Here's the question: How many grooves does the record have?

- Teach someone else. Trying to explain mathematical concepts to someone else will quickly pinpoint what you really know or don't know. It's virtually impossible to get someone else—especially someone who is slower than you at all this stuff—to understand the material if you don't.

By the way, the answer to the question about the grooves in the record is: one. If the record didn't have one continuous groove, the music wouldn't keep playing! In case you didn't notice, none of the mathematical information provided had the slightest bearing on the answer. (For those of you who aren't sure what a "record" is, a pox on your youth.)

You should approach foreign language texts the same way, especially basic texts that teach vocabulary (we'll deal with memorizing vocabulary words in the next chapter) and fundamental rules of grammar. If you haven't mastered the words you're supposed to in the first section, you'll have trouble reading the story at the end of the third.

Follow the Yellow Brick Road

When I discovered highlighters during my first year of college, my reaction was, "Where have you been all my life?" I couldn't believe how terrific they were for zeroing in on the really important material in a text. However, I soon realized that I was highlighting too much—rereading high-lighted sections became nearly the same as reading the whole darn text again.

I developed this set of rules for making the most of my high-lighters during college as my workload became much heavier:

- I highlighted areas of the text with which I didn't feel completely comfortable.

- I identified single words and sentences that encap-sulated a section's major ideas and themes.

- I concentrated on the key words, facts, and concepts, and skipped the digressions, multiple examples, and unnecessary explanations.

- I underlined or highlighted my classroom notes as well as texts to make studying from them easier.

To sharpen your underlining and highlighting skills, read through the next three paragraphs, excerpted from *Compassionate Capitalism* by Marc Benioff and Karen Southwick (Career Press, 2004), and identify the key sentence(s) or words:

At most companies, corporate philanthropy typically gets started in one of two ways. The first way occurs when the CEO gets very passionate about a particular cause and decides to donate personal and/or corporate money to it. The second way is when the company decides that it needs to do philanthropy for PR/marketing reasons and begins making grants, either through a corporate giving program or a foundation.

There are obvious flaws with both of these approaches. In the first, philanthropy never really becomes part of the culture, but is dependent upon the CEO's whim and can be turned off or on depending on his or her devotion to the cause. Even though passionate CEOs can do great things in charitable giving, there's a risk that the commitment may not survive the CEO's time at the top, especially in these days of rampant CEO turnover. Not only that, the CEO's passion may not fit well with the company's business, which again can cause philanthropy to sputter out if the CEO leaves or gets diverted by other issues.

In the second scenario, the company proclaims that it has, say, $500,000 or $1 million to give away, and is immediately inundated by requests from all sides. Every group, from schools to homeless shelters to outdoor theater companies to struggling artists, seeks a share of the largesse. The corporate philanthropy is largely reactive, responding to grant proposals, rather than proactive, putting in place a program that makes sense for the company and spelling out the types of projects it will consider. The motivation—to gain PR plaudits—is viewed as cynical by employees, so it does not engage them. Ultimately, the commitment is superficial and easily dislodged in difficult times.

Which words or phrases would you underline in this example? Here is the method I would employ.

At most companies, <u>corporate philanthropy</u> typically gets started in one of <u>two ways.</u> The first way occurs ①<u>when the CEO gets very passionate about a particular cause</u> and decides to donate personal and/or corporate money to it. The second way is <u>when the company decides that it needs to do philanthropy for PR/marketing reasons</u> and begins making grants, either through a corporate giving program or a foundation.

There are <u>obvious flaws;</u>with both of these approaches. In the first ① <u>philanthropy never really becomes part of the culture,</u> but is dependent upon the CEO's whim and can be turned off or on depending on his or her devotion to the cause. Even though passionate CEOs can do great things in charitable giving, there's a risk that the commitment may not survive the CEO's time at the top, especially in these days of rampant <u>CEO turnover.</u> Not only that, the CEO's passion may not fit well with the company's business, which again can cause philanthropy to sputter out if the CEO leaves or gets diverted by other issues.

In the second scenario, the company proclaims that it has, say, $500,000 or $1 million to give away, and is immediately ②<u>inundated by requests</u> from all sides. Every group, from schools to homeless shelters to outdoor theater companies to struggling artists, seeks a share of the largesse. The corporate philanthropy is largely <u>reactive,</u> responding to grant proposals, rather than proactive, putting in place a program that makes sense for the company and spelling out the types of projects it will consider. The motivation—to gain PR plaudits—is viewed as cynical by employees, so it does not engage them. Ultimately, the <u>commitment is superficial and easily dislodged</u> in difficult times.

With this method, if you had to review the text for an exam, you would glance at the few words you highlighted to get the gist of the three paragraphs, saving you a good deal of time.

Retention

Retention is the process by which we keep imprints of past experiences in our minds, the "storage depot." Subject to other actions of the mind, what is retained can be recalled when needed. Items are retained in the same order in which they are learned. So, your studying should build one fact, one idea, one concept on another.

Broad concepts can be retained much more easily than details. Master the generalities and the details will fall into place.

If you think something is important, you will retain it more easily. An attitude that says, "I will retain this," will help you remember. So, convincing yourself that what you are studying is something you must retain and recall increases your chance of adding it to your long-term memory bank.

As I mentioned in the last chapter, let yourself react to the data you are reading. Associating new information with what you already know will make it easier to recall.

Still Having Trouble?

If you've followed these suggestions and are still having trouble retaining what you read, try these other ideas. They are a bit more time consuming, but undoubtedly will help you.

Take Notes

Do you own the book you're reading? Do you not care about preserving it for posterity? Then use its margins for notes. Go beyond mere highlighting to assign some ranking to the facts conveyed by the text.

I used to use a little shorthand method to help me remember written materials. I'd draw vertical lines close to the text to assign levels of importance. One vertical line meant that the material should be reviewed, two indicated that the facts were very important, and asterisks would signify "learn or fail" material. I'd insert question marks for material that I wanted one of my more intelligent friends or the teacher to explain to me further. I'd use circles to indicate the information I was dead sure would show up on the next test.

Interestingly, I found that the very act of assigning relative weights of importance to the text and keeping a lookout for test material helped me remember because it heightened my attention. (For a more detailed method of taking notes, see Chapter 6.)

Become an Active Reader

Earlier in this chapter, I urged you to quiz yourself on written material to ascertain how well you'd retained it. If this doesn't work, try asking the questions before you read the material.

For instance, even though I have been an avid reader throughout much of my academic life, I had some trouble with the reading comprehension sections of standardized tests the first couple of times I attempted them. Why? I think I had a tendency to rush through these sections.

Then someone suggested to me that I read the questions before I read the passage. Presto! Great scores in reading comp (765 points on my verbal SAT for all of you doubters!).

While you won't always have such a ready-made list of questions, there are other sources—the summaries at the beginnings of chapters, the synopses in tables of contents. Pay attention to these.

For instance, if an author states in an introductory paragraph, "Containing the Unsatisfactory Result of Oliver's Adventure; and a Conversation of Some Importance between Harry Maylie and Rose," as Charles Dickens does in *Oliver Twist*, you may ask yourself:

- What was Oliver's unsatisfactory adventure?
- What could the result of it have been?
- What could Harry, Maylie, and Rose be talking about that's so important?

Believe it or not, this technique will train your mind to hone in on those important details when they arise in the story. It would also be a good idea to ask yourself these questions immediately after you finish the chapter. It will help you ascertain whether you "got" the important points of the chapter and help you retain the information longer.

Understand, Don't Memorize

Approach any text with the intent of understanding it rather than memorizing it. Understanding is a key part of memorization. Don't stop the flow of information during your reading (other than to underline and take notes). Go back and memorize later.

Organize the Material

Our minds crave order. Optical illusions work because the mind is bent on imposing order on every piece of information coming in from the senses. As you read, think of ways to organize the material to help your mind absorb it.

I always liked diagrams with single words and short phrases connected with arrows to show cause-and-effect relationships. Or I would highlight in texts the reasons things occurred with a special mark. (I used a triangle.)

Develop Good Reading Habits

It's impossible for anyone to remember what he read at 3 a.m. or while waiting to go on the biggest date of his life. Set aside quiet time when you're at your best. Are you a morning person? Then wake up early to do your reading. Do you get going at 6 p.m.? Then get your reading done before you head out for an evening of fun.

Don't forget to use your dictionary to look up terms you don't understand. (Or put the information in the next chapter to use. Then you won't need a dictionary!)

In Case You Forgot

Each time you attempt to read something that you must recall, use this six-step process to assure you'll remember:

1. **Evaluate the material.** Define your purpose for reading. Identify your interest level and get a sense of how difficult the material is.

2. **Choose appropriate reading techniques** for the purpose of your reading. If you are reading to grasp the main idea, then that is exactly what you will recall.

3. **Identify the important facts** and remember what you need to. Let your purpose for reading dictate what you remember, and identify associations that connect the details to recall.

4. **Take notes.** Use your own words to give a synopsis of the main ideas. Use an outline, diagram, or concept tree to show relationships or patterns. Your notes serve as an important backup to your memory. Writing down key points will further reinforce your ability to remember.

5. **Review.** Quiz yourself on those things you must remember. Develop some system by which you review notes at least three times before you are required to recall. The first review should be shortly after you have read the material, the second should come a few days later, and the final review should take place just before you are expected to recall. This process will help you avoid cram sessions.

6. **Implement.** Find opportunities to use the knowledge you have gained. Study groups and class discussions are invaluable opportunities to put what you have learned to good use. Participate in group discussions—they'll greatly increase what you recall.

If you find after all this work that you need still more help with reading, comprehension, and recall, I recommend *Improve Your Reading,* one of the other volumes in my *How to Study Program*.

Chapter 5

One Chapter to a Better Vocabulary

T he way to a great vocabulary is at your fingertips, and it has absolutely nothing to do with those word-a-day calendars.

In this chapter, I will show you two ways to improve your memory for sesquipedalian (having many syllables) and small, obscure words.

The Building Blocks Method

Whenever possible, try to remember concepts rather than memorizing random data. For instance, if someone told you to memorize a long string of numbers—e.g., 147101316192225—it would be far better to note that each number is three higher than the one before (1, 4, 7, 10, 13, 16, etc.) and simply remember that rule.

Similarly, it is far better to absorb the way words are con-structed—to memorize a relatively small number of prefixes, suffixes, and roots—rather than trying to cram the contents of Webster's Dictionary into your already crowded memory.

A Note on English

Our borrowed mother tongue, English, is perhaps the most democratic of all languages. Built on a Celtic base, it has freely admitted a multitude of words from other languages, particularly French, Latin, Greek, German, and a rich body of slang (from anywhere we could get it).

The oldest branches in this diverse family tree, Celtic and Old English, are the least amenable to some of the tech-niques we are about to learn. These are basically simple words, not built in complicated fashion as are Latinate and Greek terms.

However, as anyone addicted to crossword puzzles can tell you, our language is replete with myriad Romance words (those from French, Italian, Spanish, and others) that often can be dissected into rather simple elements.

The Roots of Language

Here are two dozen or so roots from Latin and Greek that contribute to thousands of English words:

Root	Meaning	Example
annu	year	annual
aqua	water	aquarium
arch	chief	archenemy
bio	life	biology
cap, capt	take, seize	capture
chron	time	chronological
dic, dict	say	indicate
duc, duct	lead	induction
fact, fect	do, make	effective
fer	carry, bear	infer
graph	write	graphics
homo	same, identical	homonym
logos	word	logical
manu	hand	manufacture
mitt, miss	send	remittance
path	feel, feeling	apathy
ped, pod	foot	pedal
plico	fold	implication
pon, posit	place, put	imposition
port	carry	export
psyche	mind	psychopathic
scrib	write	scribe
spec	observe, see	speculative
tend, tent	stretch	intention
tene,	have, hold	tenacious
vert, vers	turn	introverted

The Cart Before the Horse

As the list of root words suggests, knowing its definition alone is usually not enough. Prefixes, the fragments added to the beginning of a word, can greatly change the message conveyed by the root. Here are some examples of common prefixes:

Prefix	Meaning	Example
a-, ab-	from, away	aberration
a-, an-	without, not	amoral
ad-, af-,	to, toward	admonition
at-, ag-		affection
		aggressor
ant-, anti-	against	antidote
ante-	before	antecedent
bi-	two	bicycle
con-, com-	with, together	commitment
de-	away from	deviant
dis-	apart, opposite	disrespect
e-, ex-	out of, over	exorbitant
en-	in	envelope
extra-	beyond	extraordinary
hyper-	above, over	hyperthermia
hypo-	under	hypoglycemic
il-, im-, in-	not	illicit
		impeccable
inter-	between	intercept
intra-	within	intrauterine

Prefix	Meaning	Example
mal-	evil	maladjusted
multi-	many	multiply
ob-, op-	toward, against	obdurate
		opposite
per-	through	perspicacious
peri-	around	peripatetic
post-	after	posthumous
pre-	before	premonition
pro-	for, forth	production
re-	again, back	regression
sub-, sup-	under	substantiate
sym-, syn-	with, together	sympathetic
		synergy
tri-	three	triangle
un-	not	uncool

The Tail That Wags the Dog

The last, but certainly not the least important building block of words, is the suffix, which quite often indicates how the word is being used. Suffixes can be used to turn an adjective into an adverb (the "-ly" ending), to compare things (smallER, smallEST), or even to modify other suffixes (liveLIEST). Some suffixes with which you should be familiar are:

Suffix	Meaning	Example
-able, -ible	capable of	pliable
-ac, -al, -ial	pertaining to	hypochondriac remedial
-acy	quality of	fallacy, legacy
-age	quality of	outage
-ance, -ence	state of being	abundance
-ant, -ent	one who	student
-ary	devoted to	secretary
-cy	state of	lunacy
-dom	quality of, state of	martyrdom kingdom
-en	made of	wooden
-er, -or	one who	perpetrator
-ful	full of	woeful
-hood	state of	neighborhood
-ic	pertaining to	pedantic
-ine	like	leonine
-ion	act of	extermination
-ish, -ity	quality of	purplish enmity
-ist	one who practices	novelist
-ive	disposition of	active
-less	lacking	penniless
-ly	like	cowardly
-ment	process of	enlightenment
-ness	state of	holiness

Suffix	Meaning	Example
-ory	pertaining to	memory
-ose	full of	grandiose
-ous	like	porous
-ry	state of	ribaldry
-some	full of	toothsome

Practice Those Prefixes

Of course, I don't expect that you'll memorize these lists. But if you read them over a few times, paying particular attention to the examples, you'll absorb the roots, prefixes, and suffixes fairly quickly.

Here's a list of 20 words. Write the definition in the blank space using what you've just learned about the building blocks of words. Then check the earlier lists to see how you did.

1. Hydroponics: _____

2. Fractious: _____

3. Omniscient: _____

4. Refractive: _____

5. Pundit: _____

6. Myopia: _____

7. Voluble: _____

8. Branchial: _____

9. Consequent: _____

10. Depredate: _____

11. Thermoform: _____

12. Rheumatic: _____

13. Millilux: _____

14. Isometric: _____

15. Ketosis: _____

16. Hegemony: _____

17. Aurist: _____

18. Magnanimous: _____

19. Opalesce: _____

20. Sardonic: _____

Method with Madness in It

How did you do on the quiz? I'll bet a lot better than you thought, simply because of this rather brief introduction to etymology.

Now let's examine another way of remembering so that you can have powerful words at your disposal: the soundalike method. As we saw in Chapter 3, forming your own associations—sometimes wildly outrageous ones— can be quite helpful in carving easy-access roads to the long-term memory banks.

In order to use this method, create a scenario using the soundalike of the word or parts of the word and the definition of the word.

Consider this example: Let's say that you've seen the word "ostracize" countless times, but can never quite remember that it means "to cast out from a group." You could then create this nonsense thought: "The ostrich's eyes are so big, no one wants to look at him."

In such an example, you would be using the size of the ostrich and creating an absurd reason he might be a cast out. I could have also made the phrase: "The ostrich's size was so big he was thrown out of his hole."

Sure, you're saying, that's an easy example. But let's take another one. Since we're in a chapter on vocabulary, let's consider "sesquipedalian," which means "having many syllables" or "tending to use long words." Our soundalike association could be: She says, "Quit peddling those big words."

One picture might be worthy of a particular vocabulary word. You might associate the difficult-to-remember word not with a phrase, but with an outrageous picture.

For instance, to remember that the word "flambe" means a food covered with flames, think of a plate of food with bees whose wings are ablaze flying from it.

Again, as we learned in Chapter 3, this sort of exercise is not a lot of work, but it is a great deal of fun. It'll help your mind hold onto words, even those you use infrequently, forever.

Here's a list of "50-cent words" with soundalikes that will make them easy to learn:

Isochrous	(having the same color throughout): I so wish Chris would use one color.
Gladius	(short sword used in ancient Rome): Those gladiolas are pointy, Ron.
Fouter	(something that has no value): That router is useless.
Raki	(a liquor): Rack up those drinks.
Burgoo	(thick oatmeal gruel, eaten especially by sailors): Brrr, that oatmeal froze in the igloo.
Limner	(a person who paints or draws): Timber! The painting fell!
Triquetra	(a geometric figure with three points): You three squares better try to get bras.
Oneiric	(of or pertaining to dreams): I dreamed I was on Eric.
Clyster	(an enema): I got a blister on my butt.
Geoduck	(a large clam): Gee, is that a duck or a large clam?
Asthenia	(lack or loss of strength): Athena was weak.
Pyoidra	(a kind of Cuban sport shirt): Put on your shirt and buy me a beer, Fidel.

Tugrik	(a Mongolian coin): Two bricks, you mongrel.
Curricle	(a light, two-wheeled open carriage): Care to curl up in my carriage?
Erythema	(abnormal redness of the skin): Your red skin is eerie.
Strunt	(fleshy part or stump of a horse's tail): Look at that horse strut.
Rijstafel	(an Indonesian meal): Rice and strudel, you Indian.
Pokelogan	(stagnant water that has branched off from a stream): Poke your leg into that stream.
Radeau	(an armed scow): Don't scowl at my tatoo.

With this tool, you can become a pedantic conversationalist and never have to run to the dictionary while reading *Finnegan's Wake.*

Feel free to use any of the memory methods in this book to remember anything. If you have to remember the word "surreptitious," for example, why not combine the sound-alike and chain-link methods by picturing a burglar, black mask and all, carrying a bottle of pancake syrup?

Chapter 6

Taking Notes to Remember Text

I have a confession to make, a rather difficult one for someone whose specialty is careers and education: To this very day, I resent having to write an outline for a book, article, or research project. I'd much rather just sit down and start writing.

I would have hated myself in school if I knew then what I know now: You should do outlines while you are reading as well. The fact is, outlines will help you review a text more quickly and remember it more clearly.

In Chapter 4, I advised using highlighters to, well, highlight important messages. This is great for a relatively easy-to-remember text. For other courses, it would be a sure sign of masochism, as it assures only one thing: You will have to read a great deal of your deadly textbooks all over again when exam time rolls around.

Likewise, marginalia usually make the most sense only in context, so the messy method of writing small notes in white space around the text will engender a great deal of rereading as well.

So then, what's the most effective way to read and remember your textbooks? Sigh. Yes, that good old outline.

Reverse Engineering

Outlining a textbook, article, or other secondary source is a little bit like "reverse engineering"—a way of developing a schematic for something so that you can see exactly how it has been put together. Seeing that logic of construction will help you a great deal in remembering the book—by putting the author's points down in your words, you will be building a way to retrieve the key points of the book more easily from your memory.

Outlining will force you to distinguish the most important points from those of secondary importance, helping you build a true understanding of the topic.

The Bare Bones of Outlining

Standard outlines use Roman numerals, (I, II, III), capital letters, Arabic numerals (1, 2, 3), lowercase letters (a, b, c), and indentations to show the relationships between and importance of topics in the text. While you certainly don't have to use the Roman numeral system, your outline would be organized in the following manner:

Title

Author

I. First important topic in the text

   A. First subtopic

      1. First subtopic of A

         a. First subtopic of 1

         b. Second subtopic of 1

      2. Second subtopic of A

II. The second important topic in the text

Get the idea? In a book, the Roman numerals usually would refer to chapters, the capital letters to subheadings, and the Arabic numbers and lowercase letters to blocks of paragraphs. In an article or single chapter, the Roman numerals would correspond to subheadings, capital letters to blocks of paragraphs, Arabic numbers to paragraphs, small letters to key sentences.

We understand things in outline form. Ask an intelligent person to recount something and he'll state the main points and only enough details to make his words interesting and understandable. The discipline of creating outlines will help you zero in on the most important points an author is making and capture them, process them, and, thereby, retain them.

Sometimes an author will have the major point of a paragraph in the first sentence. But just as often, the main idea of a paragraph or section will follow some of these telltale words: therefore, because, thus, since, as a result.

When you see any of these words, you should identify the material they introduce as the major points in your outline. Material immediately preceding and following almost always will be in support of these major points.

Create a Timeline

I always found it frustrating to read textbooks in social studies. I'd go through chapters on France, England, the Far East, and have a fairly good understanding of those areas, but have no idea where certain events stood in a global context. As more and more colleges add multicultural curricula, you may find it even more difficult to "connect" events in 17th-century France or 19th-century Africa with what was happening in the rest of the world (let alone the U.S.).

An excellent tool for overcoming that difficulty is a timeline that you can update periodically. It will help you visualize the chronology and remember the relationship of key world events.

For instance, a simple, abridged timeline of James Joyce's literary life would look like this (I would suggest you create a horizontal timeline, but the layout of this book makes reproducing it that way difficult. So here's a vertical version):

1882	Birth
1907	*Chamber Music*
1914	*Dubliners*
1916	*A Portrait of the Artist as a Young Man*
1918	*Exiles*
1922	*Ulysses*
1927	*Pomes Pennyeach*
1937	*Collected Poems*
1939	*Finnegan's Wake*
1941	Death

This makes it easy to see that Joyce was born as the U.S. experienced a post-Civil War boom in industry and population growth and died during World War II. If you added other literary figures from the same period, you would not soon forget that Joyce, Virginia Woolf, Ezra Pound, W.B. Yeats, Lady Augusta Gregory, Charles Darwin, George Eliot, and D.H. Lawrence, among many others, were all literary contemporaries. Adding nonliterary events to your timeline would enable you to make connections between what was being written and what was going on in the United States, Britain, Europe, Africa, and so forth.

Draw a Concept Tree

Another terrific device for limiting the amount of verbiage in your notes and making them more memorable is the concept tree. Like a timeline, the concept tree is a visual representation of the relationships among several key facts. For instance, one might depict categories and specific types of animals in this way:

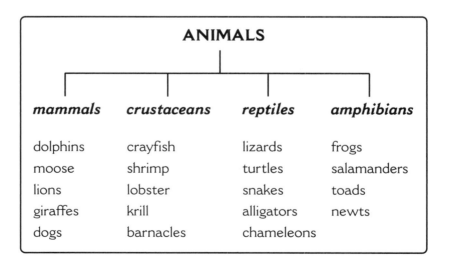

ANIMALS			
mammals	*crustaceans*	*reptiles*	*amphibians*
dolphins	crayfish	lizards	frogs
moose	shrimp	turtles	salamanders
lions	lobster	snakes	toads
giraffes	krill	alligators	newts
dogs	barnacles	chameleons	

Such devices certainly give further credence to the old saying, "A picture is worth a thousand words," because timelines and concept trees will be much more helpful than mere words in remembering material, particularly conceptual material. Developing them will ensure that your interest in the text will not flag too much.

But don't limit yourself to these two types of "pictures." Consider using a chart, graph, diagram, or anything else you can think of to reorganize any information for any class you're taking (especially the sciences, history, or English).

The more extensive and difficult the information you need to understand, the more complex your pictorial summary may have to be. Rearranging information in this way will not only show connections you may have missed, but will also help you understand them better. It sure makes review easier!

Add a Vocabulary List

Many questions on exams require students to define the terminology in a discipline. Your physics professor will want to know what vectors are, while your calculus teacher will want to know about differential equations. Your history professor will want you to be well-versed on the Cold War, and your English literature professor will require you to know about the Romantic Poets.

Therefore, as I read my textbooks, I wrote down new terms and definitions in my notes and drew little boxes around them. I knew these were among the most likely items to be asked about on tests, and that the boxes would always draw my attention to them when I was reviewing.

Most textbooks will provide definitions of key terms. If your textbook does not define a key term, however, make sure that you write the term down in your notes with its definition. Remember that your notes should reflect your individual understanding of the term. Take the time to rephrase and write it in your own words. This will help you remember it.

After you've finished making notes on a chapter, go through them and identify the most important points—the ones that might turn up on tests—either with an asterisk or by highlighting them. You'll probably end up marking about 40 or 50 percent of your entries.

When you're reviewing for a test, you should read all the notes, but your asterisks will indicate which points you considered the most important while the chapter was fresh in your mind.

To summarize, when it comes to taking notes from your texts or other reading material, you should:

- Take a cursory look through the chapter before you begin reading. Look for subheads, highlighted terms, and summaries at the end of the chapter to give you a sense of the content.

- Read each section thoroughly. While your review of the chapter "clues" will help you to understand the material, you should read for comprehension rather than speed.

- Make notes immediately after you've finished reading, using the outline, timeline, concept tree, and vocabulary list methods of organization as necessary.

- Mark with an asterisk or highlight the key points as you review your notes.

CHAPTER 7

REMBRING HOW TOO
SPEL GUD

Every time I had my daughter read to me when she was younger, I become aware of the difficulties of spelling in English. What's that "k" doing on the edge of the knife, and why didn't someone put the lights out on that "gh" in night? How come graffiti has two "f"'s and one "t," while spaghetti doubles the "t" (and pronounces the "gh" as a hard "g"!)?

Well, one way to win the spelling bee in your town is to have a great vocabulary, using some of the suggestions mentioned in Chapter 5. Another way is to learn the rules of English spelling, then note the rather frequent exceptions to those rules.

Double or Nothing

Many people make mistakes on words with doubled consonants. The most common quick-repeating consonants are "l," "n," "p," and "s", but "t" and "r" repeat fairly often, too. While the incidence of these doubles might seem accidental or arbitrary, they usually follow these rules.

Double "l": Usually results from adding prefixes ending in "l" to roots beginning with the letter, and vice versa for suffixes (examples: alliterative, unusually). However, alien does not have a double "l" because it is itself a root.

Double "n": A similar rule applies to "n"s. Double "n"s usually result from adding a suffix that turns an adjective ending in "n" into a noun (wantonness or thinness) or "-ny," which turns a noun ending in "n" into an adjective (funny).

Double "p"s, "r"s, and "s"s don't generally have a hard-and-fast rule, so you'll usually have to rely on other tricks of memory. For instance, I've always had trouble spelling embarrassment (double "r" and double "s") since it certainly doesn't seem to follow the same rule as harassment (double "s" only).

In these cases, you'll have to associate some rule with the word. When I worked as a reporter, I'd often hear colleagues answer questions about spelling in such codes. "Four 's's and two 'p's" is the answer to "How do you spell Mississippi?" I remember the rule for the word harassment by imagining someone pushing away (or harassing) the extra "r" some part of my brain insists should be there.

Double "r"s and double "t"s and other doubles occurring (note the double "r"!) before "-ed":

1. If the word ends in a single consonant (occuR, omiT).

2. If the word is accented on the last syllable (comPEL, reMIT).

Is It "i" Before "e" or...?

The general rule is: "I" before "e" except after "c" or when it sounds like "a," as in neighbor and weigh. This rule holds, with some exceptions: seize, leisure, caffeine, and the names of other chemical compounds.

Honest "-able"

Many people get thrown over words ending in "e" that have "-able" or "-ible" added to them. What to do with that final "e"? Well, here are some rules:

- Keep the final "e" for words ending in "-ice," "-ace" or "-ge." Someone is embracEABLE and situations are managEABLE.
- Drop that final "e" when it is preceded by any consonant other than "c" or "g" (unlovable).

Other rules for adding suffixes to words ending in "e":

- Retain the "e" when adding "-ly" and "-ment" (unless the word ends in "-dge." It's judgment, not judgEment).
- Drop the "e" before adding "y" as a suffix (phony).
- Drop the final "e" and add "-ible" to words ending in "-nce," "-uce," or "-rce" (producible, unconvincible).
- Use "-ible" for words ending in "-miss" (dismissible).

Affect and Effect

The general rule of thumb is that affect is a verb and effect is a noun. Since rules are made to be broken, though, effect is sometimes used as a verb.

Its vs. It's

Its is the possessive of something (e.g., its color); it's is used in place of "it is" or "it was" (e.g., it's easy).

Your vs. You're

You're is used in place of "you are" (e.g., you're tall); your is the adjective (e.g., your grades).

Plurals and Possession

If something belongs to each person, each person's name gets the 's (e.g., Jodi's and Dave's clothes, because they each have their own clothes). But if something belongs to people collectively, only the name closest to that something gets the 's (e.g., Jodi and Dave's house, because the house belongs to both of them).

Rules Are Meant to be Broken

The English language is based on Celtic, Norwegian, German, Latin, French, and several other languages. As a result, it veers from the rules fairly often. So, while these guidelines certainly will help you a great deal, sometimes you will have to rely on association and some of the other methods we spoke of in other chapters to remember all the exceptions to them.

CHAPTER 8

REMEMBERING NUMBERS THE MNEMONIC WAY

U p until now, we've been dealing in the rich world of words. Anything having to do with words is a relatively easy task for the memory because words always can be associated with things, which, because they can be seen, touched, heard, and smelled, can carry more than one association and, therefore, be easier to remember.

But a number is an abstraction. Unless associated with something, it is relatively difficult to remember. For instance, most people have tremendous difficulty remembering telephone numbers that they've only heard once. The reason is that a phone number doesn't usually conjure up an image or a sensation. It is merely a bunch of digits without a relationship to one another or to you.

The trick, then, is to establish more associations for numbers.

But how? After all, they can be so abstract. It would be like trying to remember colors without having the benefit of things associated with those colors.

Making Friends with Numbers

Numbers are infinite, but the system we use to designate them is even more user friendly than the alphabet. It consists of 10 digits that all of you know by now: 0, 1, 2, 3, 4, 5, 6, 7, 8, and 9.

The trick to the mnemonic alphabet—a rather popular technique for remembering numbers—is turning those numbers into the equivalent of letters, symbols that represent sounds. The pioneer of this concept is Harry Lorayne, author of many books on memory. His method calls for associating the 10 familiar Arabic numerals with a sound or a related group of sounds.

Here's how this brilliantly simple scheme works:

1 = T, D	6 = J, soft G, CH, SH
2 = N	7 = K, hard C, hard G, Q
3 = M	8 = F, V, PH
4 = R	9 = P, B
5 = L	0 = Z, soft C, S

You're probably thinking, "What sense does this all make, and how in heck am I supposed to remember it?"

Well, though this seems like madness, believe me, there's some extraordinarily wonderful method in it.

The number one is a single downstroke, as is the letter "T." "D" is a suitable substitute because it is pronounced almost the same way as "T"—by touching the tongue to the front of the roof of the mouth.

"N" represents two because "N" has two downstrokes.

"M" is a stand-in for three because, you guessed it, it has three downstrokes.

Four is represented by "R" because the dominant sound in the word four is the "-RRRRRR" at the end.

The Romans used "L" to represent 50. Also, if you fan out the fingers of your left hand as if to say, "It's 5 o'clock," your index finger and thumb form the letter "L."

Hold a mirror up to a six and you get a "J," particularly if you write as badly as I do. Therefore, all letters pronounced like "J"—by touching your tongue to the inside of your lower teeth—are acceptable substitutes for six.

Place two sevens back to back, turning one upside down, and what do you have? Right, a "K." All of those letter sounds formed in the back of the mouth, as is "K," are therefore potential substitutes for the lucky seven.

Draw a line parallel to the ground through a handwritten eight and you will create a symbol that resembles a script, lower case "F." Therefore, all sounds formed by placing the top teeth on the lower lip can represent eight.

Once again, I invoke my mirror, mirror on the wall to show that a nine and a capital "P" are virtually identical. "B," also formed by putting your lips together, is a substitute for nine anytime.

Zero is an easy one. Zero begins with a "Z," so any sound formed by hissing through the space between flat tongue and roof of mouth is acceptable.

Lorayne reminds us that what's important is the sounds these letters make. That's why, when using mnemonics, you assign no numerical value to silent letters nor to doubled consonants (two "tt"s are the same sound as one), unless each of the letters sounds different (e.g., accessory).

Now What?

Believe me, the mnemonic alphabet, which probably seems very ungainly to you now, is a terrific way to remember numbers. Go over the list on page 80 a few more times, cover it up, and take the little quiz below, matching numbers with appropriate sounds and vice-versa:

8 _____		K _____
V _____		7 _____
N _____		R _____
3 _____		P _____
T _____		0 _____

Consonantal Divide

Have you noticed that all of the sounds used in the mnemonic alphabet are consonants? That's because users of the system are free to use vowels however they please around these consonants to form words or memorable sounds. Therefore the number 85 can be FooL. Or the number of that wonderful person you met in the Student Center today and would so like to see again could be a "normal girl," or 2435475 (NRMLGRL).

How about trying to remember pi to seven places? You could try to memorize 3.141592 or just think, "MeTRic TalL PeNny."

Is it easier to remember your social security number (say, 143-25-7170) or "DooRMeN LiKe DoGS"?

A Great Date

One of the most useful applications of this method is remembering dates and tying them to events. If you needed to remember that William the Conqueror invaded England in 1066, you could endlessly repeat that sentence, or you could remember, "Bill THiS eGG." Combining these methods with the chain-link technique we discussed in earlier chapters, you could imagine an egg rolling off the white cliffs of Dover, where William first landed. (Alternately, you could make up a ridiculous but simple rhyme like, "In 1066, Billy C ate fish and chips.")

Now you try it. Make up phrases using the mnemonic alphabet equivalents for your social security number, the first three phone numbers in your little black book, or the times for high and low tide tomorrow. Then try the following quiz, writing in first the letter equivalents for the numbers, then a brief word, phrase, or sentence that would help you remember it. I've done the first one for you.

633020	JMMSNS	JiMMy'S NoSe
489306	_____	_____
57839462	_____	_____
925587025	_____	_____
1234567890	_____	_____
8951204736	_____	_____

What about even longer numbers? How do you remember 20-, 30-, even 50-digit numbers without trying too hard? Well, you could make your "story sentences" longer. But you could also group the numbers into a series of pictures. For example, let's say you had to remember the number 168758832427799418509079855088—that's 30 digits! Try grouping it into smaller number combinations, creating a picture for each.

> 1687588 represents The eDGe oF a CLiFF.
>
> 3242779 is MNRNGCP. Standing there is a MaN weaRiNG a CaP. (Do you see him?)
>
> 9418509 is BRDFLSB. A BiRD FLieS By. What happens next? 079855088 is SCPFLLSFF. HiS CaP FaLLS oFF.

Can you see how you could easily memorize a 50-digit number with just four or five pictures? Try it yourself. You'll see how easy it is.

Everybody Loves Them Dead Presidents

Or so sang Bluesman Willie Dixon, referring to the presidential portraits that grace our folding money. But he could just as easily have been referring to your least favorite history professor—the one who expects you to know who the 23rd President of the United States was. By the way, that was Harrison, and the way we will remember that is "No ('N' represents 2), My ('M' is for 3) hairy son."

Now you try it. Here are a dozen pretty obscure U.S. vice presidents (is there another kind?). How are you going to remember them and the order in which they served?

30. Charles Curtis

6. Daniel Thompkins

28. Thomas Marshall

13. William King

4. George Clinton

24. Garret Hobart

16. Andrew Johnson

26. Charles Fairbanks

18. Henry Wilson

5. Elbridge Gerry

20. Chester Arthur

27. James Sherman

How Did You Do?

Here's how I would use mnemonics to establish a chain link between names and numbers:

- A DoMe was built to honor the king. (13)
- The Johnsons have a DitCH in their backyard. (16)
- Will's son is DeaF. (18)
- Imagine having arthritis (Arthur) in your NoSe. (20)

Get the idea? This is an invaluable tool that will even help you remember phone numbers without having to jot them down on wet cocktail napkins. Perhaps more important, it will help you remember dates and facts without incessantly repeating them.

Where to Hang Your Memory

Another mnemonic memory method is the Peg Word System, which assigns a different word to numbers 1 through 10 (and, as Harry Lorayne describes in many of his books, can be extended right up to 100). Harry's peg words don't need to be memorized since they're based on the mnemonic alphabet you already learned:

The Peg Word System	
1. Tie	6. Shoe
2. Noah	7. Cow
3. Ma	8. Ivy
4. Rye	9. Bee
5. Law	10. Toes

When you have to remember a list in order or associate a number with some other information (such as vice presidents of the United States), you can use these peg words for the numbers. And as I mentioned previously, Harry has even extended the list to 100, utilizing words such as mummy (33), cage (76), roof (48), and dozes (100).

It's certainly possible to create your own peg word system utilizing the sounds of the mnemonic alphabet (though why reinvent the wheel Harry already designed?). Alternatively, you can utilize a completely different basic peg word system cited by author Dr. Fiona McPherson in her book *The Memory Key* (Career Press, 2000). While not associating it to the sounds used in the mnemonic alphabet, using a rhyme scheme makes it equally memorable: One is Bun, two is Shoe, three is Tree, four is Door, five is Hive, six is Sticks (or Bricks), seven is Heaven, eight is Gate, nine is Line, and ten is Hen.

As I emphasize throughout this book, use whichever method or list of peg words you find easiest, or go ahead and create your own!

CHAPTER 9

REMEMBERING NAMES AND FACES

L ike it or not, you're not going to be in school for the rest of your life. You'll soon begin to look for a job, and to string together a network of acquaintances and contacts that will help lift you onto that first rung of the corporate ladder.

You'll participate in that horrible convention called the cocktail party and other social events where you'll be expected to be charming.

Every once in a while, I go to a cocktail party, if only to remind myself why I don't do it more often. But seriously, cocktail parties give me a chance to practice a skill that I consider one of the key reasons for my earlier success as an advertising salesperson: remembering the names (and some of the other pertinent personal data) that went with the faces.

In fact, one of the principal reasons I became interested in the subject of memory improvement was that I was tired of calling people "pal" and "buddy" when I could not remember their names after they said to me, "Hey, Ron, how have you been?"

If you have as much trouble remembering names and faces as I did, don't think you're unique. There are 14 memory tasks people are most commonly concerned about, ranging from remembering important dates, where they've put something, or whether they've done something to remembering what they've read or studied. Four of them relate to identity: remembering someone's name when you see his or her face, being able to picture a face when you know a name, remembering facts about someone you've met (his or her profession, children's names, spouse's name), and associating a person with a context (knowing that the person in front of you, whose name you actually remember, is the local baker).

The following techniques will help you avoid those embarrassing cocktail party gaffes ("Oh, yeah, I meant to call you George even though I know your name is Samantha") by showing you how to link any number of names, faces, and "vital characteristics" in a story or series of pictures.

Take a Good Look

Whenever you meet someone, look him or her in the face and make special note of some outstanding feature. Does the person have a big nose? Huge earlobes? Dimples? Big, beautiful blue eyes? A cleft in the chin? A mole? A Trump-like comb over? It doesn't have to be a particularly ugly or beautiful feature—just something that sets the person apart from the rest of the people in the room.

Once you've locked in on a feature, don't stare at it, but do get your imagination working—make that feature truly outstanding by embellishing it. If it's a big nose, make it as big as a toucan's beak in your mind's eye. Dimples should be as large as craters; big earlobes should dangle on the person's shoulders.

Don't feel you have to use this technique on every person you see; it's still easier to utilize obvious clues to jog your memory. Do you see the person's spouse at the party? Remember his name? Voila! Suddenly you remember her name. Recognize someone but can't figure out why? Instead of concentrating on the person or his face, think about where you know him from. We remember people in specific contexts and may have a difficult time if we meet them outside of that context. You may have had the same guy fill your gas tank once a week for months but get confused if you suddenly see him at a baseball game. Once you remember he works at the gas station, you'll probably remember his name!

Make Sure You Got It

I remember once introducing my friend Tony to three people who, along with him, were the first to arrive at my house for a dinner party. One minute later, I went into the kitchen to fix drinks for everybody, and Tony was right at my heels. "What was the name of that brunette in the miniskirt?" he asked in a hushed voice. "Monique," I said. "How 'bout the bald guy?" asked Tony. "That's Joe." Finally, very embarrassed, Tony asked, "And what about the other woman?"

There are fleas with longer memories. But now Tony prides himself on being able to remember the names of 30 or 40 people in a room after being introduced only once.

The first thing he taught himself to do was to repeat the person's name, looking right at him or her as he did so. Tony, being a very charming guy, doesn't do this as if he's trying out for a lead role in the remake of *Being There*. He repeats the name back as part of a greeting—"Nice to meet you, Monique." "Hi Joe, I've heard a lot about you."

Using such a technique, you will not only be noting the person's name, you will be making sure that you got it right.

Think of a Link

Once you've done that, it's time to come up with some sort of link between the name and the feature that you've already exaggerated out of proportion.

I saw the most obvious example of this as a kid when a memorist appeared on a Sunday morning TV show. He was introduced to the 100 or so youngsters in the audience and repeated all of their names back to them at the end of the show. Asked how he had done it, he used the example of a boy named Tommy Fox. The boy had a dimple, said the memorist, so he imagined a bare meadow with a hole in the middle. A fox bounded through the hedge followed by hunters shouting, "Tommy Ho!"

Bingo! The name and the face were linked forever.

Too easy, you say?

There are much easier ones. Before you go too far afield creating a memorable mental picture, don't overlook the obvious. Some names are so memorable you shouldn't have to work too hard—try "Boomer" Esiason (okay, you might have to work on "Esiason") or Chip Dale (gotta love those chipmunks).

Other first or last names should automatically trigger specific pictures—a flower (Rose, Daisy, Hyacinth), a piece of jewelry (Amber, Ruby, Jasper, Opal, Pearl, Jade, Ivory), an object (Gates, Ford, Bentley, Royce, Zipper, Glass, Cross, Brook, River, Pen, Pack, Beam, Tent, ad infinitum), a profession (Tinker, Taylor, Soldier, Spy), a city or town (Clifton, Springfield, Austin, Houston, Dallas, Savannah, York), a familiar street, the name of your favorite team, or a breed of dog or cat.

Some names differing by only a letter could use such objects as links—Pack to remember Gregory Peck, Pen for Sean Penn, Tent for Trent, Road for Rhodes, even Tombs for Thomas and Cow for Cowher. (Go, Steelers!)

Your associations could take advantage of your own particular knowledge. Small for Klein, if you know German; tie-ins to your favorite sports figure, movie star, or author; an association with terms endemic to your profession. The list of possible tie-ins is absolutely endless.

If you still can't think of such a link, you can always rhyme: Wallets for Wallace, Georgie Porgie, Bad Chad, Freaky Frank, Ron weighs a ton.

Once you've come up with these soundalikes or pictures, find some way to link them with the image you've formed of the person's chief facial features.

For instance, once I was introduced to a man named Vince Dolce (pronounced Dole-see). As I was walking toward him, I noticed some rather dark circles under his eyes. In my imagination, because I'm so accustomed to using the technique outlined above, the circles became bigger than a raccoon's. When I heard that his name was Dolce, I immediately thought, "dull sheep" and pictured tired, sleepy sheep grazing on those now even bigger circles below Vince's eyes. The sheep, of course, were bothering him, and this made him wince (for Vince).

That's all there is to turning a room full of strangers into people that—for better or worse—you'll never forget!

CHAPTER 10

LET'S NOT FORGET ADD

Just what is ADD? It's probably easiest to describe as a person's difficulty with focusing on a simple thing for any significant amount of time. People with ADD are described as easily distracted, impatient, impulsive, and often seeking immediate gratification. They have poor listening skills and have trouble doing "boring" jobs (like sitting quietly in class or, as adults, balancing a checkbook). "Disorganized" and "messy" are words that also come up often.

Hyperactivity is more clearly defined as restlessness, resulting in excessive activity. Hyperactives are usually described as having "ants in their pants." ADHD is a combination of hyperactivity and ADD.

According to the American Psychiatric Association, a person has ADHD if he or she meets eight or more of the following paraphrased criteria:

1. Can't remain seated if required to do so.
2. Easily distracted by extraneous stimuli.
3. Focusing on a single task or play activity is difficult.

4. Frequently begins another activity without completing the first.

5. Fidgets or squirms (or feels restless mentally).

6. Can't (or doesn't want to) wait for his turn during group activities.

7. Will often interrupt with an answer before a question is completed.

8. Has problems with chore or job follow-through.

9. Can't play quietly easily.

10. Impulsively jumps into physically dangerous activities without weighing the consequences.

11. Easily loses things (pencils, tools, papers) necessary to complete school or work projects.

12. Interrupts others inappropriately.

13. Talks impulsively or excessively.

14. Doesn't seem to listen when spoken to.

Three caveats to keep in mind: The behaviors must have started before age 7, not represent some other form of classifiable mental illness, and occur more frequently than in the average person of the same age.

Characteristics of People with ADD

Let's look at the characteristics generally ascribed to people with ADD in more detail.

Easily distracted. Since ADD people are constantly "scoping out" everything around them, focusing on a single item is difficult. Just try having a conversation with an ADD person while a television is on.

Short, but very intense, attention span. Though it can't be defined in terms of minutes or hours, anything ADD people find boring immediately loses their attention. Other projects may hold their rapt and extraordinarily intense attention for hours or days.

Disorganization. ADD children are often chronically disorganized—their rooms are messy, their desks a shambles, their files incoherent. While people without ADD can be equally messy and disorganized, they can usually find what they are looking for; ADDers can't.

Distortions of time sense. ADDers have an exaggerated sense of urgency when they're working on something and an exaggerated sense of boredom when they have nothing interesting to do.

Difficulty following directions. A new theory on this aspect holds that ADDers have difficulty processing auditory or verbal information. A major aspect of this difficulty involves the very common reports of parents of ADD kids who say their kids love to watch TV and hate to read.

Daydreaming, falling into depressions, or having mood swings.

Take risks. ADDers seem to make faster decisions than non-ADDers.

Easily frustrated and impatient. ADDers do not suffer fools gladly. They are direct and to the point. When things aren't working, "Do something!" is the ADD rallying cry, even if that something is a bad idea.

Why ADD Kids Have Trouble in School

What should you look for in a school setting to make it more palatable to a son or daughter with ADD? What can you do at home to help your child (or yourself)?

- **Learning needs to be project- and experience-based,** providing more opportunities for creativity and shorter and smaller "bites" of information. Many "gifted" programs offer exactly such opportunities. The problem for many kids with ADD is that they've spent years in nongifted classroom settings and may be labeled with underachieving behavior problems, effectively shutting them out of the programs virtually designed for them! Many parents report that children diagnosed as ADD, who failed miserably in public school, thrived in private school. What's usually different about these schools? They inevitably boast smaller classes and feature more individual attention with goal-setting, project-based learning methods. These factors are just what make ADD kids thrive!

- **Create a weekly performance template** on which both teacher and parent chart the child's performance, positive and negative.

- **Encourage special projects for extra credit.** Projects give ADDers the chance to learn in the mode that's most appropriate for them. They will also give such kids the chance to make up for the "boring" homework they sometimes simply can't make themselves do.

- **Stop labeling them "disordered."** Kids react to labels, especially negative ones, even more than adults. Saying "you have a deficit and a disorder" may be more destructive than useful.

- **Think twice about medication,** but don't discard the option. Many professionals are concerned about the long-term side effects of drugs normally prescribed for ADDers. However, if an ADD child cannot have his or her special needs met in a classroom, not medicating him or her may be a disaster.

Specific Suggestions for Remembering

- **Practice, practice, practice** the memory techniques in this book. ADDers tend to have trouble listening and are easily distracted. As a result, they may fail to remember things they simply never heard or paid attention to. Work on the visualization techniques. Practice making mental pictures when having conversations, create mental images of your "to-do" list, and visualize doing things to which you've committed or for which you are receiving instructions or directions. Practice careful listening skills. Many of Harry Lorayne's memory books (especially his classic, *The Memory Book* [Ballantine Books, reissue edition, 1996]), which stress "picture-oriented" approaches to memory problems, would be invaluable additions to any ADDer's library.

- **Write everything down.** This is something I recommend everyone do, but it is absolutely essential for ADDers. The more you write down, the less you have to remember!

- **Utilize pictures, mapping, diagrams,** and so on in lieu of outlines or "word" notes—even the abbreviations and shorthand I've recommended in other books.

- **Tape-record lectures** (again, despite what I wrote in *How to Study*). This will enable them to relisten and reprocess information they may have missed the first time around.

- **Create distraction-free zones.** Henry David Thoreau (who evidently suffered from ADD) was so desperate to escape distraction he moved to isolated Walden Pond. Organize your time and workspace to create your own "Walden Pond," especially when you have to write, take notes, read, or study. ADDers need silence, so consider the library. Another tip: Clean work areas thoroughly at the end of each day. This will minimize distractions.

- **Train their attention span.** ADDers will probably never be able to train themselves to ignore distractions totally, but a variety of meditation techniques might help them stay focused longer.

A special thank you to Thom Hartmann, author of many books on ADD and ADHD, for allowing me to paraphrase his suggestions in this chapter.

CHAPTER 11

TEST YOUR PROGRESS

As promised, I'm going to give you a chance to prove to yourself how much you've learned. If you've studied the contents of this book thoroughly and have made an effort to put some of its advice to work, you should score much higher now than you did on the quiz in Chapter 2.

Test 1: The Mnemonic Alphabet

Study this number for 30 seconds. Then cover it up and replicate as much as you can, taking only another 20 seconds or so.

937150387499628536

Test 2: A Better Vocabulary

Here are a number of obscure vocabulary words and their meanings. Study them for no more than three minutes, then answer the questions that follow.

Folia	A wild Portuguese carnival dance
Hypaspist	A shield bearer
Inlier	A rock outcropping surrounded by younger rocks
Combe	A narrow valley or hollow
Eloign	To remove to a distance
Heteroclite	Irregular or abnormal
Gossoon	A boy (Irish)
Raclette	A cheese dish
Wolframite	A mineral
Repoussoir	A figure or object in a painting's extreme foreground
Osmund	A fern
Jimjams	Extreme nervousness
Thaumatugy	The working of miracles
Macula	A spot or blotch
Umbriferous	Casting shade
Volvulus	A twisting of the intestine
Porphyry	A hard, purplish-red rock
Nisus	A striving toward a particular goal
Kist	A money chest
Stomatology	The science dealing with the mouth and its diseases

Okay, cover up the vocabulary list and take this test:

1. If you were on vacation and feeling feisty, you might do a _____ and throw some money around from your _____.

2. But if you were afraid, you might just _____ yourself to a quiet _____.

3. A _____ might be part of a _____ in the Arizona desert.

4. Being Irish, the _____ wasn't interested in eating _____.

5. In ancient Mesopotamia, being a _____ was an honor.

6. If you had a large _____ on your face, it would definitely be considered _____.

7. Curing a _____ would not be considered _____.

8. If you studied _____ in college, your _____ might be to become a doctor.

9. The royal variety of the _____ is not _____.

10. Don't get the _____ just because you have to handle some _____. It won't bite!

11. The _____ in Warhol's paintings was usually himself.

Test 3: Dates and Events

Study the following dates, events, and facts. Then take the test on the next page.

- William Pryor's term as Attorney General of the state of Alabama expired January 2007.
- On March 4, 1917, Jeanette Rankin became the first elected woman to take a seat in the U.S. House of Representatives.
- Dmitri Donskoi defeated the Tartars in 1380 and became the Grand Duke of Moscow.
- William Howard Taft arrived in the Philippines in 1901 to become its first U.S. governor.
- Only Maine and Massachusetts celebrate Patriot's Day (the third Monday in April), in memory of the Revolutionary War battles of Lexington and Concord.
- Pearl Buck won both the Nobel Prize in Literature (1938) and the Pulitzer Prize (1931).
- Fifty-six percent (56%) of college students are women.
- The U.S.S.R. won the most total medals at the 1984 Winter Olympics—6 gold, 10 silver, and 9 bronze—though East Germany won 3 more gold.
- Australian aborigines call their native food "bushtucks," which includes game such as turkey, kangaroo, and lizard.

- The British surrendered Singapore to the Japanese on February 15, 1942.

- More than 2,700 languages and 7,000 dialects are spoken throughout the world, with 1,000 separate languages on the African continent alone.

- Balder, the Norse god of light and son of Odin, was slain by Hoth at the instigation of Loki.

- The ambulance was created for Napoleon's Army in 1792.

- Zephon was a fallen angel (a "hell's angel") who tried to set fire to heaven.

- The Sacagawea golden dollar (which contains no gold) was introduced in January 2000, replacing the Susan B. Anthony dollar, which had been in circulation since 1979.

- Francis Hawkins wrote a manners book for children in 1641…when he was 8 years old.

- Tiger Woods was named after his father's friend, Vuong Dang Phong, who was also nicknamed "Tiger."

- The Tokyo-Osaka bullet train, which reached a top speed of 130 mph, made its first run in 1964.

- Cholesterol is transported through the bloodstream in molecules called lipoproteins.

- The distance between the horns of Babe the Blue Ox, storied companion of Paul Bunyan, was said to be 42 axe handles…and a plug of tobacco.

Questions

1. When was the ambulance created and for whom?
2. When did the British surrender Singapore?
3. How many states do not celebrate Patriot's Day?
4. What did Zephon try to do?
5. When did William Pryor's term expire?
6. What are three potential ingredients of bushtucks?
7. How many years was the Susan B. Anthony dollar in circulation?
8. Who defeated the Tartars and when?
9. Along with a plug of tobacco, how many axe handles would be needed to span the distance between Babe's horns?
10. What friend of his father's was Tiger Woods named after?
11. Lipoproteins transport _____ through the _____.
12. How many years elapsed between Pearl Buck's two awards? What were they?
13. _____ encouraged _____ to slay _____, the son of _____.
14. What percentage of college students are men?
15. How many gold medals did East Germany win in the 1984 Winter Olympics?
16. How many languages and dialects are there throughout the world?

17. In 1901, what position did William Howard Taft assume, and where?

18. What was the top speed reached by the bullet train in 1964?

19. Who was the first woman elected to the U.S. House of Representatives?

20. What kind of book did Francis Hawkins write... and when?

Test 4: Reading Retention

Scan the following paragraphs excerpted from *The World War II 100* by William Weir (Career Press, 2002), in order to answer the questions that follow (which you may read first). The answers are at the end of Test 6. This should take you no more than two minutes:

September 1, 1939, was a pivotal date in world history: Adolf Hitler invaded Poland, igniting World War II. It was also the date that George C. Marshall became U.S. Army Chief of Staff. At the time he took office, the U.S. Army ranked 19th in size among the world's armed forces, and that included its reserves. It had more men under arms than Bulgaria but fewer than Portugal. Before he was done, Marshall would build the U.S. armed forces to more than 8.5 million, fighting on many battlefields around the world. Marshall's superb leadership, his absolute integrity, his dedication to the job at hand, his attention to detail, his ability to choose talented leaders for warriors, and his grasp of global strategy made him indispensable to the war effort. Ironically, that very set of skills may have cheated Marshall of the one thing he wanted most: to lead the Allied armies into battle on the continent of Europe.

It had taken Marshall 16 years to win his first star as a brigadier general (in 1936). Three years later, he was wearing four. A strong believer in air power, he lobbied for strengthening the Army Air Corps. In 1940, he began building the army using the Selective Service Act, though it was scheduled to expire in October of 1941. That summer, throughout the country, the letters O.H.I.O. ("Over the Hill in October") were scrawled on the walls of many barracks. Yet war was imminent, and Marshall knew it. The SSA had to be extended. It appeared that the Senate would pass the extension, but there was concern about the House of Representatives. Marshall personally spoke to congressmen who were either opposed to or ambivalent toward the measure. As a result, the draft extension was approved in the House by a single vote.

As war approached, Marshall was involved in numerous issues, from national security to army morale. Roosevelt wanted England strengthened to defend itself against a German invasion. As the chief of staff, Marshall signed off on sending supposedly outmoded rifles to the beleaguered British at the same time some American servicemen were drilling with broomsticks. Upset at the sight of recruits wandering around the small towns near their training camps because they had nothing to do when off duty, Marshall came up with the idea of entertaining them; the United Service

Organizations (USO) was born. Marshall reviewed the lists of his generals, choosing those for retirement so that younger men could step forward to command. Most importantly, Marshall met with his British counterparts to plan for future military operations.

Questions

1. How long did it take Marshall to accumulate four stars?
   A. Four years
   B. Ten years
   C. Nineteen years
   D. Sixteen years

2. To what size did Marshall build the armed forces?
   A. 190,000
   B. 1.9 million
   C. 8.5 million
   D. 5.8 million

3. What did O.H.I.O stand for?
   A. Oh, Help In Oregon
   B. Ohio
   C. Over the Hill in October
   D. Over the High Occident

4. When did Marshall become Chief of Staff?

A. September 1, 1942

B. September 1, 1939

C. 1942

D. 1939

5. When was the Selective Service Act scheduled to expire?

A. September 1, 1939

B. September 1, 1942

C. September, 1941

D. October, 1941

Now read the following passage from *The Know-it-all's Guide to Life* by John T. Walbaum (Career Press, 2003) and answer the questions that follow (but do not look at the questions first). Give yourself four minutes to read the passage, two minutes to answer the questions.

In the not-so-distant future, just about anybody in good physical shape will be able to go into space—anybody that is, with $100,000 in spare cash. Although NASA has not yet bought into the concept of consumer space travel, private American companies (and possibly the Russians soon after) expect to offer suborbital flights for amateur astronauts before the end of 2005.

Space Adventures of Alexandria, Virginia is offering seven-day packages culminating with a two-and-a-half-hour flight into space. The tickets, which cost $98,000 and require a hefty deposit, are reported to be selling rapidly. During the trip, amateur astronauts will feel the pull of multiple G-forces on takeoff and reentry, and be able to clearly see the curvature of the Earth, though not the great blue marble as seen from the moon. The space trip will feature a two and a half minute period of weightlessness, during which tourists will do aerial backflips on videotape...that is, if the trip ever takes place.

If a ride in space costing $600 per minute seems a little ridiculous to you, just wait a few years. Robert Bigelow, who is president and owner of the Budget Suites of America motel chain, believes in the future of space travel. He has committed $500 million towards the construction of a 100-passenger, half-mile-long luxury cruise ship that will orbit the moon (presumably at a lower cost).

British entrepreneur and balloonist Richard Branson— a man with a nose for opportunity as well as publicity— wants to get into the act with Virgin Galactic(!) Airways. Former astronauts, like Buzz Aldrin, are also pushing to take the masses to space. There is even a course taught, at the Rochester Institute of Technology, called "Space Tourism Development," to train the next generation in space hospitality management.

Perhaps the real future is in space vacations. A joint study by NASA and the Space Tourism Association estimates space travel and tourism could be a $10- to $20-billion market. Bigelow Aerospace, also owned by Robert Bigelow, is exploring the construction of space hotels that would be partially assembled on Earth and carried into space for final assembly.

But don't pack your bags yet; the cost to launch anything into space is still prohibitive. NASA's space shuttle costs work out to about $10,000 per pound to put satellites into orbit, and rockets aren't much cheaper. Bigelow Aerospace believes launch costs need to fall to $550 per pound before space hotels become a reality.

A California company, Space Island Group, thinks it has the solution: a space station built from used external fuel tanks left in orbit by space shuttles.

If big space hotels are not cost effective, how about a little orbiting bed and breakfast? MirCorp, a Netherlands-based company that attempted to salvage the Mir space station, hopes to launch a tiny space station for tourists. The space bungalow, to be called Mini Station 1, will hold only three visitors at a time. Bring your own Tang.

On the other hand, if you have $20 million, you can now reserve a seat aboard the Soyuz rocket, like tycoons Dennis Tito and Mark Shuttleworth, who lodged at the orbiting International Space Station. All you have to do is learn to speak Russian and spend six months training at the Gagarin Cosmonaut Training Center in Star City, Russia. Space Adventures, which also offers rides in Russian military aircraft, is brokering the trips.

Even if space hotels do not become a reality in your lifetime, don't be too chagrined. Space cabins are not exactly the Ritz-Carlton—or even a Budget motel, for that matter. Simple activities like using the toilet, bathing, and eating are a chore in space. Although the food is no longer served in squeezable tubes, as it was on the early Apollo missions, it has more calories than flavor (think TV dinners).

Weightless sleep is reported to be heavenly, but 70 percent of astronauts experience space motion sickness (symptoms include nausea, vomiting, and headaches) in response to micro-gravity. The body's reaction to weightlessness also means strenuous daily exercise is required to keep muscles from atrophying.

Microbes thrive in the closed environment of a space cabin, making staph infections and other illnesses common. It's expected space visitors would be given a complete physical exam and quarantined prior to take-off to reduce the risk of infecting other travelers. Even with filtration systems aboard, a crowded cabin can stink to high heavens from stale air and body odors.

Another appetizing thought: Scientists expect longer space trips will mandate "closed systems," meaning that all water aboard the spacecraft —including human waste—will be purified and reused. Furthermore, as the Challenger shuttle disaster made clear, the odds of a fatal catastrophe in a space trip are enormous. They are estimated by NASA to be about 100 to 1, or 70 times higher than the odds of dying in an automobile accident this year.

If you don't have the money or live long enough to see the price come down, there is one more way to get to space. For just $5,300, Celestis Inc., of Houston, Texas, will launch a portion of your cremated remains into low-Earth orbit. If you were truly destined for the moon, for $12,500 Celestis will deliver your ashes to the Sea of Tranquility aboard NASA's Lunar Prospector satellite.

Questions

6. Who is Robert Bigelow?
   A. President of a Ritz Carlton
   B. Owner of Bigelow Rockets
   C. Both A and B
   D. Neither A nor B

7. What are the odds of your dying in an automobile accident this year?
   A. 1,000 to 1
   B. 7,000 to 1
   C. 100,000 to 1
   D. 70,000 to 1

8. What percent of astronauts experience space motion sickness?
   A. 10%
   B. 7%
   C. 70%
   D. 700%

9. At what cost does at least one company believe space hotels would become feasible?
   A. $70,000 per pound
   B. $10,000 per pound
   C. $550 per pound
   D. $1,000 per pound

10. Where is the "Space Tourism Development" course offered?

A. M.I.T

B. R.I.T

C. Rochester Polytechnic Institute

D. Rochester Institute of Aeronautics

Test 5: Remembering Lists, However Obscure

Study the first two lists for two minutes each, then close the book and recite them back. Do the same for the third and fourth lists, except allow five minutes to study each of them:

British monarchs: Eadwig, Aethelred, Svein, Canute, William I, Stephen, Charles I, Anne, George III, John, Edward V, Henry VII, Mary I, Elizabeth, Richard I, Egbert.

Desert plants: Hedgehog, elephant tree, devil's claw, chuparosa, desert paintbrush, smoke tree, apache plume, mojave aster, wooly daisy, ghost flower, soaptree yucca, mormon tea, showy milkweed, yellow beeplant.

Norse mythology: Yggdrasill, Bragi, Frigga, Asgard, Jotunheim, Nidavellir, Ginnungagap, Ragnarok, Loki, Midgard, Aegir, Balder, Fulla, Vidar, Tyr, Utgard, Nifleim, Hodur, Ratatosk, Ymir.

Egyptian pharoahs: Menes, Djer, Djet, Den, Anendjib, Semerkhet, Qa'a, Reneb, Ninetjer, Peribsen, Sanakhte, Khaba, Huni, Snefru, Khufu, Merenhor, Nikare, Ibi, Imhotep, Isu, Neferkare,Pepi, Yoam, Amu, Heribre, Ined, Hori, Bnon, Apophis, Yakbam, Sekhanre, Rahotep.

Test 6: The Rules of English Spelling

Identify the mispelled words in the following list:

eventualy	seperate	harrass
supersede	parallell	independant
reccomend	acommodte	dillemma
comparitive	ocurrence	profesion
ethinic	ilnesses	broshure

How did you do? (See the bottom of this page for the answers to Test 4 and the spelling solutions.)

I hope that you scored well and are confident that you can approach your schoolwork—and the rest of your life, inside and outside of school—with the assurance that your memory will be an ally rather than a foil.

Test 4 answers: 1) C, 2) C, 3) C, 4) B, 5) D, 6) D, 7) B, 8) C, 9) C, 10) B.

In the previous list, every word is spelled incorrectly, including "mispelled." Got you!

INDEX

Notes

Notes

About the Author

Ron Fry is a nationally known spokesperson for the improvement of public education and an advocate for parents and students playing an active role in strengthening personal education programs. In addition to being the author of the vastly popular *How to Study Program*, Fry has edited or written more than 30 different titles — resources for optimum student success.

"Helpful for students of all ages from high school and up."
– Small Press Book Review

"These are must-read guides every family should have in its library."
– Library Journal

How to Study Series:

- **How to Study**
- **Ace Any Test**
- **Get Organized**
- **Improve Your Memory**
- **Improve Your Writing**
- **Improve Your Reading**

For product information and technology assistance, contact us at

Cengage Learning Customer & Sales Support,
1-800-354-9706.